FB
4 95

4 95

Be a
PUPPETEER!

Be a

PUPPETEER!

THE LIVELY PUPPET BOOK

written and illustrated by
ESTELLE ANSLEY WORRELL

McGRAW-HILL BOOK COMPANY
New York · Toronto · London · Sydney
St. Louis · San Francisco · Mexico · Panama

For

Steve W., Sue, Steve A., Anne,
Buzz, Elizabeth, Shannon, David,
Rick, Clare, Sherry, Bryan, Sterling,
Scott, Clay, and Shawn

Library of Congress Catalog Card Number: 76-91689

1234567890   HDEC   754321069

CONTENTS

chapter 1

Plan to Be a Puppeteer

FIRST OF ALL, just what is a puppet? A puppet is a figure of a person, an animal, or an object which is made to move by the efforts of a human being. If motors or batteries or the wind make the figure move, then it is not really a puppet. Whatever the puppet depicts, it must be given life, or manipulated, by a *real live person.*

The person who manipulates or works a puppet is a puppeteer. A puppeteer can move his puppet with just his hands or with strings, rods, or levers. This book is concerned with simple hand puppets, sometimes called glove puppets because they slip over the hands. We will use rods on some of them for hand-and-rod puppets.

Puppetry is among the oldest forms of theatre in the world. Puppets performed for an audience long before people-actors did. The first puppets were made for a religious or magical purpose. Probably a clever medicine man thought of putting a lever or a crank or string on a statue to make it move and then he convinced people that the spirits made it move! After a time the medicine men realized that people enjoyed seeing the statues move, and they began to make them dance or eat or move to entertain the people.

We know that ancient Egyptians had puppets because string-operated clay figurines have been discovered by archeologists in more than one Egyptian tomb. The Greek historian, Herodotus, who visited Egypt in the fifth century B.C., described a puppet that was used as part of a religious ceremony there and he said that puppets were already ancient then!

Animated religious statues have also been found in the ruins of Greece and Rome. In fact, the word "puppet" comes from the Latin *pupa* which means "small creature or doll."

Bernal Diáz del Castillo, a member of Cortez' expedition to Mexico, mentioned in his diary that Cortez brought a puppeteer and musicians with him into Mexico. He also wrote that the Indians already knew how to work them because they used puppets themselves in religious ceremonies.

It is generally agreed by historians that in primitive tribes, religious masks came first, then movable masks. Later, when bodies were added to the movable masks, the puppet was born.

In some countries today puppets are used to help both children and adults learn about politics and other serious subjects. Puppetry can be a good teaching tool, but the kind of puppetry we will be concerned with in this book is just for fun. Puppetry is theatre and even though it can be sad or serious it must, first of all, entertain.

When a puppet makes the audience laugh, he does so more by what he *does* than by what he says. The words that the puppeteer makes the puppet say are not nearly as important as the way he makes the puppet's body move, makes his face show emotion, and the way he makes him act in everything he does on stage.

Puppetry is almost entirely visual in India, where traveling puppeteers have been going about the country giving shows for hundreds of years without ever using words. However, they do use sounds such as squeaks, grunts, whistles, and cries. India has many small villages and the people of one village may speak a different language than the people of another only a few miles away. The puppeteer can travel from one village to another to give his shows and not have to worry about what language is spoken in each village.

Even after all these centuries of tradition in the art of puppetry we are still learning new things about puppets. Every puppeteer, no matter how young, can learn from the puppeteers before him, add new things he learns and then pass the traditions on to future young puppeteers.

When you plan your own show, remember to keep it simple. Sometimes beginning puppeteers want to use microphones, large stages, colored lights and elaborate scenery in large auditoriums before they have learned to be good puppeteers. There is nothing wrong with wanting to make your show a big production later on but right now it is important to concentrate on becoming a good puppeteer because all the technical gadgets in the world won't help a show that has uninteresting puppets.

The best place to give a show is in a classroom, a corner of a library, your own room or den, or any medium-size room. If you should want to give your show to a large group such as a whole school, it works best to repeat it several times to small groups, to two grades at a time perhaps. The audience can sit on the floor around and up close to the puppet stage if you like.

Once I had to give my shows in a large gymnasium so I borrowed a large rug and rolled it out on the floor in front of my stage which I had put in a corner. I told the principal I would give the show to as many students as could sit on the large rug at a time. They came all morning, two classes at a time, to see the show and it was a great success! The warm rug on the cold gym floor and the corner in which the stage had been set up gave everyone a feeling of coziness even though we were actually in a huge room.

Don't be afraid to tell people how you want things arranged for your show. After all, if you are willing to go to the trouble to produce the show, then you should make sure that you give it in a place which will allow you to do your best.

You are going to find that if you really go all the way and complete your show, rehearse it well, and let people know about it, you will be asked to perform over and over again.

One of the very best places to give your show is at birthday parties. Parents are always looking for clever ways to make a party special. I've had many requests, through the years, to give shows at parties, but there has never been enough time to fit them all in. My two older daughters, Anne and Elizabeth, hated to see me miss a performance. That's what made them decide to try it. Now they give shows every month. They enjoy doing them and they love the wide-eyed amazement of the young audiences. They have fun and make extra spending money at the same time!

That brings me to the very reason for telling you about puppetry. Puppetry is exciting, and the better a puppeteer you are, the more fun it is. I want above all else to share with you what I've learned so that you can have fun being a puppeteer too!

chapter 2

Select Plays to Suit You and Your Audience

BE A PUPPETEER. Why use this title instead of LET'S MAKE PUPPETS or GIVING A PUPPET SHOW?

To be a puppeteer means being and knowing many things—not just how to make your own puppets and puppet-stages—it means knowing about which plays to choose, and about the different kinds of audiences who will come to see the puppet show. It means always remembering that every audience which takes the time to see a show deserves to be entertained.

A good puppeteer observes people and animals and learns to put what he sees into his puppets so that they become "living" creatures during a play. He observes each audience so closely that eventually he can sense, during a performance, how they feel about the play. He learns that he can add something here and there, or leave out something, speed the action or slow it down, and make each performance something special for each audience.

Most of all, being a puppeteer means being a part of the theatre and feeling very proud of sharing ideas with others by actually giving a puppet show.

After you have decided that you want to be a puppeteer, the first thing you must do is select a story to use for your play.

How do you know whether a story will be good for a puppet play? Ask yourself these questions; your answers will tell you.

1. Am I going to be the only puppeteer? If not, how many others are going to help? How many hands will there be?

2. Does the play I am considering give my puppets plenty to do, such as picking up or holding things, walking, fighting, cleaning house, etc., so that they will be fun to watch? Or is the play mostly talk, talk, talk?

3. Are there props in the play that will give my puppets things to do and give the audience more to watch? Are there too many props?

4. Who will come to my puppet show? Will they be very young, school age, or grown up?

Now let's answer these questions one by one.

■ 1. *Am I going to be the only puppeteer? If not, how many others are going to help? How many hands will there be?* If you are going to be the only puppeteer you will have to think about the number of characters because you have only two hands. It doesn't matter how many characters the story has—what does matter is *how many must be on stage at the same time.* You must consider that you can never have more than two puppets on stage at a time. With two puppeteers you can have as many as four on at a time. Two people can always work a show more easily than one, but you can manage by yourself if you plan your show well. You wouldn't plan to give a play such as "Snow White and the Seven Dwarfs" with just two hands, would you?

When you have fewer puppeteers than characters, the solution is to have someone work with more than one puppet; but when you have more puppeteers than characters, another problem arises. This is likely to happen when you have a group such as a Scout troop, school class, Sunday school class, or neighborhood gang, planning a show. If there are twice too many people, then give two short shows instead of one. If you have only one or two extra people, there are several parts they can take.

For one, you can always use a puppet announcer or master of ceremonies who gives the title and announces things like "scene one" or "the end." He can introduce the characters for a curtain call and so on. Boys often like this part.

For another, you can add certain characters to the play without changing the plot or story. A cat, dog, bird, mouse, or other animal can join almost any play. You don't want to overdo this adding of characters. It's better to give another play if you have too many extras.

By the way, if you are going to have another person help you, make some decisions first. Decide who should play what parts and have your puppets ready. You can always change your mind, or be persuaded by a friend, but you should have some plans in mind. Someone needs to be in charge. Since you are making the effort, you be the director—but remember that there are many ways of doing things. The suggestions of others can be helpful.

———————————◆———————————

■ 2. *Does the play I am considering give my puppets plenty to do, such as picking up or holding things, walking, fighting, cleaning house, etc., so that they will be fun to watch? Or is the play mostly talk, talk, talk?* An audience wants to *see* the show as well as listen to it. A good puppeteer could give the three plays in this book without speaking a word and even very young children could understand them.

The two skits with Marian the Librarian and Dewey the Bookworm would be difficult to do without words though, because they are more about ideas.

When you read stories from now on you will find yourself thinking, "Boy, this would be great for a puppet show!" or "This story is too hard for hand puppets to act out."

Simple stories with lots to look at, such as "The Gingerbread Man," are easy to make into plays. Fables, like "The Tortoise and the Hare" or "The Swollen Fox," and Bible stories, such as "David and Goliath," are good to start with.

———————◆———————

■ 3. *Are there props in the play that will give my puppets things to do and give the audience more to watch? Are there too many props?* Usually, the stories that are the easiest to make into plays have to have the most properties (objects other than the puppets). Because there is more to see in a simple visual play, there will naturally be more things for the puppets to hold, to make, or to look at. Happily, young puppeteers like to use props! The props give the puppets something to do. They have to pick them up, throw them, hold them, swing them, and so on. The props automatically decide some of the action for you. This makes the play easier for beginners.

Some plays can require too many props. For example, "The Three Bears" is a delightful story and an easy one to write dialogue for, but at the same time it requires so many props (such as chairs, beds, bowls, and coats) that it is a problem to produce.

———————◆———————

■ 4. *Who will come to my puppet show? Will they be very young, school age, or grown up?* The age of your audience should be considered when you plan your show. If you are going to give the show for kindergarten, it must be short and have plenty of action. If you want a longer program for young children, it is better to plan two short shows than one long one.

Think seriously about each audience and learn to plan your show to fit the audience and the occasion. A group of senior citizens will be a different audience from a group of Boy Scouts, or a Sunday school class will be different from a paying audience at a school carnival. Not only will the audiences differ in personality but they may differ physically too. You might give a show to an audience who are sitting in wheelchairs or sitting up in beds spread out over a large area, or you might give it for young children who are sitting close together on the floor very close to the stage.

When your audience is very, very young—only 2, 3, or 4 years old—you can have a puppet that is not in the play talk to them for a moment at the beginning about how to behave at a puppet show. Sometimes you need to explain that they should stay seated and not come up to touch the puppets during the play. If you want to, you can have the puppet tell your young audience that you will show them the puppets after the play.

There are many ways to make the audience feel that you wrote the show just for them. Find a place in the dialogue to put in the name of the group seeing the show. Watch for other opportunities to make your audience feel special.

chapter 3

Three Plays and How to Write Your Own

As YOU WORK with puppets and make new ones to add to the ones you already have, you are naturally going to think of ways to use these puppets in new plays. Sooner or later, you are going to think about writing your own plays!

If you happen to have several animal and people puppets, you can make just one new one—a gingerbread man—and have all the characters for a new play. The new puppet can run across the fields and through the forest meeting various animals who can't catch him. You can use your wolf for a fox if you need to and have him eat the gingerbread man. You can write the play to fit the animals you already have and still use the same plot.

Seasonal puppets, such as Santa Claus or an Easter bunny or a jack-o'-lantern, get stored away for most of the year, but my daughters and I worked out a play for them which can be used any time. Here it is:

It is a birthday party, and you are going to give a show as part of the entertainment. Out on the puppet stage comes a puppet who can't remember what is special about today. (It's the birthday, of course.) The puppet knows it's an important day but he just can't think what day it is. The audience will invariably tell you very excitedly because they are so pleased to know something the puppets don't know.

Santa comes in with his bag of toys and says something like, "Ho, ho, ho, Merry Christmas!" Then he looks puzzled and says, "Why aren't you in bed?" The first puppet answers, "Ho, ho, ho, yourself. It's not Christmas yet, Santa!"

Santa then explains that he has been working so hard that when he heard everyone trying to guess what day it was he jumped into his sleigh and dashed off thinking he had let Christmas slip up on him.

13

A witch can think it is Halloween, a bunny can start hiding his eggs, a turkey can look for a hiding place, and so on—whatever holiday puppets you happen to have can be used. The lines can be turned around to fit any special day of the year. You don't really need a script because you already know the puppets and special days so well.

This play can even be planned around the important days concerning one particular religion, nationality, or race as long as your audience is familiar with the facts.

There are possible plays everywhere if you just look around. Do be careful though, that you don't become too serious. A pilgrim puppet can tell about the first Thanksgiving and he can be truly grateful when he gives thanks, but he could first have a wild chase with a turkey or perhaps an Indian. He can catch the turkey, or the turkey could catch him, or the turkey catch the Indian—you can see the possibilities. Perhaps at the meal right at the end of your play when the audience assumes the turkey is being eaten, the turkey can enter and join the family—who turn out to be eating ham or fish or something else because the pilgrim couldn't catch the turkey. Do you see what I mean?

Audiences want puppets to be clever, mischievous, clumsy, stupid, forgetful, very bad, very good, very . . . *anything*, but not dull and serious. *You will get your message across to the audience better when you have funny moments in between the serious ones.*

"THE THREE LITTLE PIGS"

I chose this play for your first production because the story is well known, and it's best to use a play based on a familiar story when you first start. If you forget your lines, you can quickly make up new ones without changing the story. It takes longer to learn lines when a story is new to you. Once you learn the first scene in this play you can do the second scene because the words are practically the same. The third scene is almost the same until the wolf huffs and puffs.

Another reason for starting with this play is that you not only repeat the dialogue, you repeat the puppet patterns too. You need only two kinds of puppets, a wolf and a pig. You can make the other two pigs the same way you made the first, using different colors and clothes, of course, so the audience can tell right away that each is a different pig. You can give this play all by yourself because you never need more than two characters on stage at a time. Although two hands are enough, you can have another puppeteer help you if you like.

If you have too many puppeteers you might add other characters without changing the outcome of the play. You could have one of the pigs, as he enters with his bundle of straw, meet another animal and tell him how he is going to build his house. This other animal can talk to him and ask questions while he works, then say goodbye and exit before the wolf enters.

"THE THREE LITTLE PIGS"

SCENE I

1ST PIG
I think I'll build me a house so I'll be safe from the big bad wolf. I think I'll build it of—let me see—straw! I'll build my house of straw!

(*He leaves, then returns with straw and begins to "build" house.*)
Dum de dum, "Home, home on the range."
(*Continues to sing or hum as he reaches to get straw, puts it on house, bends down to get more straw, puts it on house and so on. As he adds the straw, you slowly raise house a little bit at a time. Remove bundle of straw from stage during the building so it won't be there when house is finished. When house is the proper height [you should be able to see it through the curtain], hook the pin into the curtain so the house will stay in place.*)
There—it's finished! Let me see, it needs a picture.
(*Goes off stage, gets picture, returns, and hangs it in place. If it takes more than one try to hang picture, don't worry—it will make it funny. He brushes his hands off, then exits, gets broom, returns, and sweeps floor.*)

WOLF
(*Let him come in slowly from side of stage. He looks all around starting with the audience, while the pig sweeps. Let him slowly turn his head around toward the pig's house. When he sees the house, let him jump suddenly and say:*)
Aha!, I'll have a pig for dinner tonight!
(*Have the wolf do much smacking and licking of his chops greedily.*)
Oh little pig, little pig, come out.

1ST PIG
No, no, not by the hair of my chinny-chin-chin.
(*Shakes head when he says "no, no."*)

WOLF
Little pig, I have an apple for you. Come out, and you may have it.
(*Exits, and gets apple. Holds it in mouth for a moment. Exits and removes apple. Enters. If you have a shelf at the stage opening, just have wolf put the apple down on it.*)
It's ripe and delicious.

1ST PIG
No, no, no . . .

WOLF
(*Angrily*)
If you don't come out, I'll huff and I'll puff and I'll blow your house down.

15

1ST PIG   No, no, no. . . .

WOLF   (*Opens mouth wide, moves back while you make a noise with your own mouth as you inhale. Then blow, making a sputtering, blowing noise with your lips closed as the wolf closes his lips and moves toward the house. The more noise he makes the funnier it is. Remember, the wolf should be so bad that he is funny.*)

1ST PIG   (*Holds onto the house and shakes it so that the house appears to shake from the wolf's huffing.*)

WOLF   (*Blows again in the same way.*)

1ST PIG   (*Remove the house by raising it a little, then let it appear to fall over sideways. Although you will have to have the pig hold the house to remove it, it will look as if he is holding onto the house to keep from being blown away.*)

WOLF   (*For an instant, after the house and the pig are gone, have the wolf turn to the audience with his mouth hanging open as if he is a little bit amazed at his own strength! This will give you time, also, to put the house down and return the pig for the chase. Have the wolf chase pig across stage. Open and close his mouth as he moves up and down. The pig should bob with short, quick, up-and-down movements.*)
            Heh, heh, heh,
            (*Laughs wickedly.*)

SCENE II

2ND PIG (a girl)   I think I'll build me a house so I'll be safe from the big bad wolf. I think I'll build it of sticks.
            (*Exits, then returns with a bundle of sticks. Puts it down and begins to build house.*)
            Dum de dum . . .
            (*Continues to sing or hum as she reaches to get stick, puts it on house, bends down to get more sticks, puts them on house, and so on. As she adds the sticks, you slowly raise the house a little bit at a time. When the house is the proper height [you should be able to see it through the curtain], hook the pin into the curtain so the house will stay in place.*)
            There—it's finished! Hummm, a little dusty though.
            (*Goes off stage, gets feather duster and begins to dust the house.*)

WOLF   (*Appears at the side of the house and looks in just as the pig goes

16

by dusting. She dusts the wolf's face. Let the wolf turn and look at the audience and wrinkle up his nose in disgust and then sneeze. He turns back toward house and says:)
Aha! I'll have pig for dinner tonight after all.
(Smacks lips greedily.)
Ah little pig, little pig, come out.

2ND PIG   No, no, no, not by the hair of my chinny-chin-chin!
(Shakes head.)

WOLF   If you don't come out, I'll huff and I'll puff and I'll blow your house down!

2ND PIG   No, no, no.
(Shakes head.)

WOLF   *(You inhale and then blow noisily for him with sputtering as in the first scene.)*

2ND PIG   *(The pig should hold onto the house and shake it.)*

WOLF   *(Blows noisily again in the same way as before.)*

PIG   *(Remove house by raising it slightly while shaking it. Then move it over sideways so it appears to fall as the wolf blows again, as in the first scene.)*

(Exit with wolf chasing pig.)

SCENE III

3RD PIG   *(Whistles as he enters carrying bricks.)*
I want to build a house that's safe and strong. So I'll build it of bricks.
(Begins to build house as before and sings:)
"Mortar and bricks
Stronger than sticks,
Stronger than straw
As you just saw. . . .
I'll build a fire, good and hot.
I'll put the water in the pot.
Just keep on looking . . .
You'll see the wolf cooking!
Mortar and bricks,
Mortar and bricks."
(When house is pinned in place, says:)

17

There!
(*Brushes off hands.*)
It's finished! Now to build a fire.
(*After building an imaginary fire have him warm his hands at the fire and say:*)
Ah, just right for cooking!

WOLF   Oh little pig, little pig, come out.

3RD PIG   (*Jumps back, puts hands to mouth.*)
No, no, no, not by the hair of my chinny-chin-chin.
(*Shakes head very confidently.*)

WOLF   Little pig, little pig, come to the fair with me.

3RD PIG   No, no, no.

WOLF   (*Angrily*)
Come out or I'll huff and I'll puff and I'll blow your house down.
(*Blows several times, then hangs head over edge of stage and pants. Blows again, then pants and gasps in exhaustion!*)

3RD PIG   My house is strong; it's made of bricks. You can't get me . . . with your old tricks!

WOLF   (*Turns to audience and says:*)
I'll go up to the roof and come down the chimney, heh, heh, heh.
(*Exits*)

3RD PIG   (*Have him hum:*)
Who's afraid of the big bad wolf?
(*while you are getting the wolf into position.*)

WOLF   (*Unseen behind curtain.*)
Ho, ho, ho, here I come!
(*Say this loud and clear so he sounds as though he really is on the roof. Stick his head up under the curtain and through the fireplace opening and yell:*)
Yowwwww!

3RD PIG   (*Turns to audience and sings happily:*)
Who's afraid of the big bad wolf?

WOLF   (*Remove him from the fireplace, then let him return on stage with a sign in his mouth which reads:*)

THE END

"LITTLE RED RIDING HOOD"
(with Marian and Dewey)

"Little Red Riding Hood" is one of my oldest plays. My children have worn out two wolves through the years—the poor villain has been battered up so many times! When I began to do some serious research into the history of puppetry a few years ago, I found out, to my surprise, that puppeteers have been doing this play for many, many years. It seems that practically every puppeteer has done his own version of this old fairy tale at some time or other.

Puppetry is one of the oldest forms of theatre, and I hope that you will feel some excitement about doing *your* very own version of a story which has become traditional in one of our oldest arts.

The story in my play has a new story added to it to make it a play-within-a-play. With Marian and Dewey the play is more than just a fairy tale. Young people can learn something while they are having fun.

When we try to teach with puppetry we have to be careful not to make our audience feel that we think they are ignorant, but it's funny to them when Dewey is "igernent." The audience can learn something new when Marian teaches Dewey and they aren't insulted because, after all, isn't it Dewey who needs to be taught?

By the way, can you guess why I named the bookworm Dewey? Well, you know those numbers that are put on the spines of books in the library so that you can find the book you want? The system of using those numbers is called the "Dewey Decimal System," so what else could I call my bookworm but Dewey!

The play is written so that you can use all of it for young people and adults or only the "Little Red Riding Hood" part for very young children.

With this play, "Little Red Riding Hood," you will learn a lot about voices and character. You will have to do a very deep, wicked voice for the wolf and then do a voice which is a wolf-imitating-a-little-girl. This should not be the same voice as the sweet, soft, little-girl voice. Then later you have to do a wolf-imitating-a-grandmother voice which should be different from the grandmother voice.

The more you practice the funnier the play will be. You will find, when you first begin to rehearse, that you will forget sometimes to change voice and be speaking in the wrong one! Don't worry, everyone does this at first. If you should do it during your performance remember that the play is absurd anyway, so do your best and have fun.

The audience will never believe that the awful, big-mouth wolf really is a grandmother—that's what makes it funny! Maybe this is one of the reasons why this story has been done by so many puppeteers. Each character is so different from the others and so much himself that one can *pretend* to be another and the audience still knows exactly who each one is!

If you need to add a character or two because you have more puppeteers than characters you can have Little Red Riding Hood meet and talk to animals in the forest such as a skunk, rabbit, or squirrel. They can either help to delay her trip

19

or they can warn her of the dangers and try to hurry her on, whichever you prefer.

Since this is a *play-within-a-play* it is simple to make it suit your audience. The entire play is written for audiences who are old enough to learn about fiction and non-fiction. If your audience is very young it probably will be best to use just the fairy tale part. If your audience is school age then they will enjoy and perhaps learn something from the library scenes.

"LITTLE RED RIDING HOOD"
(with Marian and Dewey)

SCENE I: A library

MARIAN, LIBRARIAN   (*Enters with a note pad in hands. Puts it down, exits to get a large pencil, then returns and starts to write as she says:*)
Let me see, we need two new copies of "The Fairy Tale Book" and one new copy of . . .

DEWEY, BOOKWORM   (*unseen*)
Yawn
(*Makes a yawning sound from backstage, loud enough for the audience to hear.*)

MARIAN   (*Stops, looks all around, then continues to write.*)
Now where was I? Oh yes, one new copy of . . .

DEWEY   (*still unseen*)
Yawnnnnnn, smack, smack.
(*He sticks his head out from behind his book just as Marian looks in the opposite direction.*)

MARIAN   (*Turns slowly toward Dewey's book, meets Dewey face-to-face, jumps, and screams:*)
Eeeeeeeeek! What is it!

DEWEY   Dahhhh, I'm a worm, a bookworm to be exact. My name is Dewey. And might I ask, who are you? Huh?

MARIAN   A bookworm, well my stars! Whatever are you doing in that book?

DEWEY   Oh, just nibbling and resting.
(*Looks at audience.*)
What else is there to do in a library?

MARIAN   My goodness gracious! You are uneducated, aren't you!

DEWEY   Dahhhhh, yep.

20

(Nods head "yes.")

MARIAN   Oh, by the way, I'm Marian and I'm the librarian. Do you mean that you just waste all your precious time doing nothing but eating! Why, you could be traveling around the world or out into space, learning things, doing things, READING things!
(She uses her hands as she tells him this and his eyes follow her hands.)

DEWEY   Ya mean I could read a book, huh, maybe?
(Looks at audience as if to ask them, too.)

MARIAN   By all means! Now let me see, what is a good book for you? How about fiction?
(She puts her hand to her chin as she thinks.)

DEWEY   *(Opens mouth, looks at audience, then back at Marian.)*
Fickshun, ahhh—what's that?

MARIAN   You are ignorant, aren't you?

DEWEY   *(Nods "yes," then "no," then "yes" again.)*

MARIAN   Fiction is "something invented by the imagination or feigned; an assumption of a possibility as a fact irrespective of the question of its truth . . ."

DEWEY   *(Interrupts Marian with:)*
Ahhhhh yeahhhh . . . well, I'll be seeing you.
(Goes back behind his book.)

MARIAN   Wait! Don't go.
(Dewey puts head out slowly as she explains.)
Let me put it another way. You see, fiction is a made-up story out of your imagination.

DEWEY   Oh I see! Like what you tell the teacher when you don't have your homework!
(Turns to audience mischievously.)

MARIAN   Ah hem! Hummmm, let me see. A fairy tale, that's it! Make yourself comfortable and . . .

DEWEY   *(As Marian talks have Dewey put his head down on the edge of the stage opening to get comfortable.)*

MARIAN   . . . and I'll tell you a fictional story about an animal who acted like a human being, though not a very good one,
(Shakes head "no.")

21

and talked and everything. Once upon a time there was a little girl who wore a red cape and hood who was called RED RIDING HOOD. . . . (*Emphasize the title as you say it.*)

(*Marian and Dewey exit and scene changes.*)

SCENE II: Forest

(*The play "Little Red Riding Hood" begins:*)

MOTHER   Yoo hoo! Red Riding Hood. . . .
(*Looks around.*)
Red Riding Hood! Are you ready to take the basket of goodies to your granny?
(*She looks to side of stage as Red Riding Hood enters from the other side.*)
Oh! there you are!

RED RIDING HOOD   Yes, Mother, I'm all ready to go.
(*Carrying a basket*)

MOTHER   Be sure to stay on the path, now, you hear? And go quickly so you can get there before dark.

R. R. H.   Yes, Mother, goodbye now.
(*Kisses her mother goodbye.*)
(*She starts walking with a short, quick, side-to-side movement. She walks across stage, Mother exits, and she turns and walks back to center of stage, turns, walks toward back curtain, humming or singing as she walks. You must take your time here and give the impression that she is walking some distance. If you use a back curtain with a forest scene, you slide it into place when she first starts walking and Mother exits. She picks a flower and smells it. The wolf enters behind her as she does this.*)

WOLF   Aha!
(*He says this loudly and quickly and it frightens her so that she jumps and throws the flower up in the air.*)

R. R. H.   (*Screams*)
It's a wicked wolf!
(*Runs to side of stage and covers face with hands.*)

WOLF   (*Looks at audience.*)
A basket of goodies—hummmm . . .
(*Looks at Red Riding Hood.*)
Good day, little girl. Where are you going with that basket?

R. R. H.	Good d-d-day. I'm going to my grandmother's to take her some goodies. She isn't feeling well today, the poor dear.
WOLF	(*Sniffs at basket greedily, looks around as if to think.*) Where does your granny live, my dear? Heh, heh, heh.
R. R. H.	Oh, *everybody* knows where my granny lives. She lives in the little pink cottage by the waterfall.
WOLF	Ah . . . that cottage. Hummmmmm, well, run along, child, so nice to have met you.
R. R. H.	So nice to have met you, Mr. er . . . uh . . . Good-bye. (*She exits.*)
WOLF	(*Looks at audience.*) Heh, heh, heh. I know a short-cut to that cottage, heh, heh, heh.

(*Exits.*)

SCENE III: Grandmother's house.

GRANNY	(*In a whiny, scratchy voice.*) My, I do feel poorly today. My back aches. (*Places hand on side.*) My knee's acting up again. (*Sighs.*) Tsk, tsk, tsk. (*Shakes head.*) Life is so hard when you are old.

(*A knock at the door.*)

GRANNY	Wh-who's there? (*Be sure to have her look in the direction of his entrance.*)
WOLF	(*In a high voice trying to imitate R. R. H. from backstage.*) It is I, Granny. May I come in? I brought you some goodies.
GRANNY	Bless my soul, child, how nice! Just lift the latch and walk right in.
WOLF	(*Enters*) Heh, heh, heh.
GRANNY	(*She screams and starts to run around the room. Use the back-to-front rocking walk. Have wolf right behind her. He catches her nightgown in his mouth and drags her offstage. She returns and runs across stage again with wolf right behind her.*)

23

(Now, while you are removing Granny, putting the wolf's nightcap on, and putting R. R. H. on your hand, squeal and stomp floor or gently kick stage and have granny yell:)
Let me out of this closet, you beast! Help, help!
(Have her yell things at the wolf until you get your puppets ready. Don't feel you must have the wolf back on stage immediately. A slight pause in the action with only sound effects will add to the suspense. Remember that the wolf's entrance in the nightcap is one of the highpoints of the play. Wolf appears slowly in nightcap and hangs his head over stage front, looks all around at the audience in a very conceited way.)

WOLF Don't I look just like Granny? Heh, heh, heh, ain't I purty?

(A knock at the door.)

WOLF Who's there?
(In a high wolf-like voice trying to imitate Granny's.)

R. R. H. It is I, Granny, Red Riding Hood. I brought you some goodies.

WOLF Well, bless my soul, child, how nice of you. Just lift the latch and walk right in.
(Looks at audience.)
Heh, heh, heh.
(Licks and smacks lips.)

R. R. H. Hello, Granny.
(Goes over to wolf, looks closely at him, then looks at audience, then at wolf again, and says:)
Goodness gracious, Granny dear, what big eyes you have!

WOLF The better to see you with, my dear.
(R. R. H. should back up a little as the wolf says this.)

R. R. H. *(Goes closer.)*
My, what very long ears you have!

WOLF The better to hear you with, my dear.

R. R. H. And Granny, what huge teeth you have!

WOLF *(In his own voice)*
All the better to eat you with!
(He goes toward her, opening and closing his mouth. She runs across stage with her same movement as before and he follows her. They can turn and run across stage again. If you are doing the play alone, you will have to exit R. R. H. and put the woodchopper on your hand

at this point. If you do this, have the wolf enter running with the woodchopper behind him.)

WOODCHOPPER *(Enters, stops, looks at audience.)*
I'll save you!
(Then continues the chase, hitting the wolf with the club.)
Take that, and that, you beast!

WOLF Help, help, lemme go, ouch!
(After he has run and yelled for a time, you can hang his head over the edge of the stage as he gets weaker.)

WOODCHOPPER How dare you, you fiend!
(Wolf goes limp and woodchopper turns away to leave.)

WOLF *(Raises head up once more. Woodchopper stops, looks around, and goes back to hit him once more. He stays limp this time. Remove your hand from inside the wolf but leave him hanging limp over the edge.)*

(Enter R. R. H.)

R. R. H. Oh, my hero!
(She hugs the woodchopper, then he exits. He need not exit if someone is helping you.)

GRANDMOTHER *(In her own voice)*
Let me out of here!
(You say this from backstage.)

R. R. H. *(She exits to get Grandmother from the closet. They both enter.)*
Thank heaven, you're safe. Let's have a tea party.
(Let them eat the goodies.)

(They all exit.)

(Have the wolf return with a sign in his mouth which reads: THE END*)*
(Marian and Dewey enter.)

DEWEY Oh boy! that was a good story! Tell me another one, will ya huh, will ya?

MARIAN Oh Dewey, dear, I'll tell you another story, but not right now. There are hundreds of books with wonderful tales for you to read. They are all around us. There's a whole world of books to be read!

(They bow and exit.)

THE END

"THE LION AND THE MOUSE"
(with Marian and Dewey)

You should produce at least one of the other plays before you attempt this one. Although you need to be a little more experienced to try this one, you will enjoy doing it. Your audience will be fascinated with the double movement of the lion puppet. Many people are not familiar with this type of puppet and if you don't let your audience see him before the show they will wonder how on earth you make him so "alive." My daughters and I are always asked to explain the lion after our shows.

You will find the way that works best for you in each show you do. This show must be done by at least two puppeteers. My daughters and I prefer to have one person do both soldiers and the mouse. The puppeteer who works the mouse can do both soldiers because they never appear at the same time the mouse does. This show is suitable for two, three, or four people.

One of my reasons for using this play is to give you the experience of producing a show and directing other puppeteers to work with you. Remember that in the theatre there must be only *one* director. If you are that director, then decide how you want to do the scenes and show the others how you want them done. If someone else is the director, then do the scenes the way he or she wants them done. You will be a better puppeteer after your group experience. Don't be afraid to change your mind. Don't be shy about changing the play. If you feel you can improve it—do it! There are as many ways to do the play as there are puppeteers who want to do it.

If you want to be really absurd you could, instead of having the lion groom himself as a lion would, have him do it with a real comb and perhaps a mirror! You can even make him appear very vain and pleased with himself and put a crown on his head when he finishes. Any age audience would enjoy this, especially a school age one.

However you decide to have the lion clean himself before going to sleep, don't rush through it. There is very little dialogue in this scene but it is a favorite one with audiences and can be short or long depending on how you interpret it. Because there are so many ways to treat this scene it is a good opportunity for you to see how you can give the puppet character with body movement and facial expression but with a minimum of words.

"THE LION AND THE MOUSE"
(with Marian and Dewey)

(Remember—you need not use the part about Marian and Dewey if you don't want to. You can use just the lion and mouse play by itself.)

26

MARIAN, LIBRARIAN   (*Nervously*)
>Oh dear, I promised to tell a story to a group of boys and girls today.
>(*Here you can actually name the particular group watching the show.*)
>I spent so much time putting the letters on the backs of all those books that I let the time slip by . . . Oh dear, they'll be here any moment and I don't know what I'm going to tell them.
>(*She wrings hands, frets, and paces as she talks. She can have a handkerchief attached to her hand and wipe her nose and eyes.*)

DEWEY, BOOKWORM   (*Sticks head out from book, looks around, is startled a little at seeing Marian.*)
>Ahhhhh, what's the matter, Miss Marian? Don't cry—ole Dewey will help you.

MARIAN
>Oh Dewey, you're so sweet, but you are just a bookworm. How could you help me?

DEWEY
>Wellllllll,
>(*Looks at audience, and all around.*)
>Ahhhh Dahhhhh,
>(*He's thinking hard. Close your fingers so he bites his lips and wrinkles his nose.*)
>I've got it! Merember when you first found me eating the books back when I was igernent?

MARIAN
>Yes, Dewey.
>(*Looks up from crying and puts hand with handkerchief down away from face.*)

DEWEY
>And you told me about all the wonderful books to read?

MARIAN
>Yes.
>(*Nods head "yes."*)

DEWEY
>Well, I read one called "Aesop's Fables." And there's a good story in it about a great lion and a little insig, insig . . .

MARIAN
>Insignificant?

DEWEY
>Yeah, that's what I said, in-sigy-niffy-sent mouse. Well, this here great lion did him a favor and then later this in-sigy-niffy-sent mouse . . .

MARIAN
>Oh Dewey, dear, you are like that sweet little mouse. I remember that fable very well.

DEWEY
>Let's tell it to them, okay?

MARIAN	First, may I tell you something about a fable? It is a story, usually about animals and people, which teaches a lesson.
DEWEY	Yep, yep. (*Nods head enthusiastically.*)
MARIAN	A long time ago a man named Aesop told these stories to people. He understood that nobody likes to be told to his face that he has acted wrong or dumb.
DEWEY	Yeah, that could be embarrassing. (*Nods head as he confirms this.*)
MARIAN	Well, when Aesop told his stories he used animals as the characters—and because the story was about animals it could not be about a man who was listening, could it? And nobody need be embarrassed while he learned the lesson and enjoyed the story. But let's tell the story. Once upon a time there was a great lion who was king of all the animals . . .

(*Marian and Dewey exit.*)

SCENE II

(*The play, "The Lion and the Mouse," begins.*)

LION	(*Licks paw and stomach. After cleaning himself he gets sleepy.*) Ho, hum, I think I'll take a nap. That was a big meal I just ate. (*Yawns, rests head on paw at edge of stage.*) Oh, I'm so sleepy. (*Stretches, sighs, chomps lips, changes position several times, then begins to snore.*) Snore . . . snore . . . bz bzzzzz . . . (*An imaginary bee comes along and lights on nose. He swats at the bee, then changes position and goes back to sleep.*)
MOUSE	Tum de dum, whistle . . . (*He walks right up over the lion's back, then over his head and down his paw, happily singing all the way. His walk should be in tiny, quick bobs.*)
LION	(*Wakes up, looks at this bold mouse and, just after the mouse steps down from his paw, lifts his paw and grabs the mouse.*)
MOUSE	(*Turn the rod so that he does a "double take" look at the lion.*

	When he struggles to free himself, just turn the rod back and forth and he will struggle in a very realistic way.) Help, help!
LION	*(Picks mouse up in paw and gets a closer look.)* Aha, caught you! How dare you walk over me, a lion, the king of the jungle! *(He holds mouse farther away as he says this.)*
MOUSE	*(In praying position, pleading.)* Pl-pl-please let me go, Mr. Lion. Don't eat me.
LION	*(Looks at mouse closely, then at audience, then back at mouse.)* And why not?
MOUSE	I'm just a little mouse who runs around on the ground and you are a great lion. I'm not worth eating, I'm so small—and besides, I might even get your great paw dirty.
LION	*(He opens his paw to see if it's dirty and the mouse jumps out! Realizing what he has done, he looks at audience, then at his empty paw, then at mouse.)* You are awfully small, aren't you? *(Looks at audience as though trying to decide, then shrugs and says:)* Oh all right! Scat! Get along before I change my mind and eat you!
MOUSE	Thank you, thank you, *(This should be very corny as he kisses the lion's paw, smacking loudly. He keeps on saying:)* thank you, thank you, thank you.
LION	Oh shoo! Scat! *(Pushes the mouse away with the back of his paw.)* Wphew . . . *(Yawns again and goes back to sleep.)*

SCENE III

(While lion sleeps, two Roman soldiers appear in back carrying spears and a net.)

| AUGUSTUS | *(He halts and Disgustus bumps into him and pokes him from behind with his spear.)*
Hup, two, three, four. Halt, Owww! Shhhhhhhhh! |

DISGUSTUS	(*Turns and sees lion sleeping—jumps and hugs Augustus and shakes with fear.*) There's a lion! Get him, get him!
AUGUSTUS	Shhhhhhh.
LION	(*Changes position as the soldiers hide at the edge of the stage. When he settles down, the soldiers return and lay their spears down. Disgustus holds the net.*)
AUGUSTUS	OK. Ready, one, two, three . . . throw it!
DISGUSTUS	(*Throws the net over Augustus instead of over the lion.*)
AUGUSTUS	Watch out, you dumbbell! You numbskull, you—you—you—. Not me—the lion! Uh, oh, shhhhh. (*Gets very still.*)
LION	(*Raises head, rubs eyes, looks around.*) I thought I heard something. Hummmm, guess I just had a bad dream.
AUGUSTUS	Now! This time get HIM, you imbecile!
DISGUSTUS	One, two, three . . . got him!
LION	(*Roars*) What the . . . Oh no, I'm caught! (*Struggles*) What an embarrassing thing to happen to the king of beasts!
AUGUSTUS	Come on, let's get the ropes and the cage and tell the general we caught a big one! (*They leave as lion moans and struggles.*)
DISGUSTUS	(*Let Disgustus look back and then bump into the side of the stage as they exit.*) Yeah, let's hurry, I don't think this lion is too happy about being caught.

SCENE IV

LION	Oh me . . . Oh me . . . Oh me . . . (*Struggles*)
MOUSE	La de da—la de da do . . . (*Walks over lion as he did in first scene, stops, then backs up, turns around, and jumps and puts hands over mouth in surprise.*)

30

	Oh! What's this! Well, you've sure got yourself in a mess, Mr. Lion.
	(*Examines the situation all around as he says this.*)
LION	Shhhh. Can you help me, friend?
MOUSE	You were kind to me once and did not eat me when you could have, so I will help you now, my friend!
	(*Starts to chew on ropes in net.*)
LION	Hurry, hurry! I hear the soldiers coming!
MOUSE	(*Makes loud chewing noises. Pants over front of stage and looks over shoulder. Chews again. Pants and looks over shoulder.*)
LION	Hurry, please!
MOUSE	(*Chews and pants some more.*)
	There! It's chewed through! You're free!
	(*Takes net off lion with the lion's assistance.*)
	Hurry, run!
	(*Exits with lion swaying from side to side and mouse bobbing in short quick bobs.*
	Soldiers return.)
AUGUSTUS	Halt!
	(*Disgustus bumps into him and pokes him with his spear again.*)
	Owww!
	(*Turns and hits Disgustus.*)
DISGUSTUS	(*Looks where the lion had been, gasps, and covers mouth.*)
	He's gone!
AUGUSTUS	It's all your fault, you nitwit.
DISGUSTUS	It is not, it's your fault, you know-it-all.
	(*They start hitting each other and then exit, still calling each other names.*
	Lion and mouse enter.)
LION	(*Reaches out and gets mouse in paw and licks him with long strokes of his tongue.*)
	Slurp, slurp, thank you, slurp . . .
MOUSE	Aw shucks, you're welcome.
	(*Turn the rod back and forth as mouse struggles to get loose.*)
	Aw come on now, you're getting me all wet!

(*They turn to audience, bow and exit.*)

THE END

(*This is a perfect place for the puppeteer who likes to sing to use a song very effectively. The two can sing the song "Friendship."*)

(*Marian and Dewey return.*)

DEWEY   That's my favorite fable, Miss Marian. Tell it to me again, will ya, huh?

MARIAN   Oh Dewey, I'll tell it to you again another day.
               (*She puts her hand on Dewey's head and gives him a little kiss.*)
               Thank you so much, I don't know what I would have done without you.

DEWEY   Ahhhh shucks . . . it's like Mr. Aesop said, "You're never too insig . . . uh . . . you're never too little or unimportant to help someone else."
               (*Looks at audience.*)
               I gotta go read another book, 'bye.

THE END

chapter 4

Make Your Own Puppets Without Sewing

THERE ARE TWO BASIC kinds of puppets shown here—those which have a body or dress with a head added on, and those which are complete puppets with head and body all made at one time. There is also a third kind of puppet—the tube and sock puppet; these puppets have mouths which can open and close.

The first reason for giving several different patterns is that a puppet show is more interesting if there is more than one kind of puppet in it. A show in which all the puppets moved in the same way might not be too interesting. Some puppets, such as the wolf, just need to be made a certain way. A mean wolf needs a big mouth; he wouldn't be funny or as interesting made in any other way. Red Riding Hood would not be dainty and feminine with such a big mouth and besides she needs hands for holding her basket.

I have made suggestions on each set of directions or patterns for the characters which are best for each particular type of puppet. You will add ideas of your own as you work with the puppets. Just follow my directions and use my patterns in the beginning while you are still learning; then after you have made several puppets, begin to design your own.

You can sew the puppets either by hand or on a sewing machine. If you prefer not to sew, you can glue the seams instead. A white liquid glue (such as Elmer's Glue-All) works best. Use a bottle with a pointed dispenser cap so that you can put the glue on in a line of dots. That is the secret of glueing. If you put the glue on in a solid line, the seams will be stiff and scratchy and just won't work. The seams made with a line of small dots will bend and stay soft like a seam which has been sewn. You can leave the puppet to dry for an hour or two after you glue it or, if you want to work on it right away, you can use a medium-hot iron and iron the seam dry in a few minutes. Be sure to put an old cloth or paper under and on top of the puppet so you won't get glue on the ironing board cover

33

or iron. (Be sure, also, to check with an adult before using the iron.) Try not to get blobs of glue on the seam—just a line of small dots as I've shown on the patterns and directions. You might try a glued seam first on a scrap of cloth to see how it works before you do it on the puppet. (You can't glue fur cloth very well.)

Whether you sew or glue you still need to clip the cloth at the curves. The puppet won't turn right side out properly unless you do this. It is a simple thing to do and the patterns show exactly where the clips are needed. They need to be tiny clips made with your scissors point—don't cut too far or you may cut past the seam and make a hole in it.

Some of the puppets in the patterns and directions section require no sewing at all and practically no glueing either! The first two given, the one made from an old shirt sleeve and the one made from a circle of cloth, for example, need glue only for the face and hair. These puppets can be made quickly and easily by even the youngest puppeteer. The sock puppet and the puppet body made from a half-circle with a styrofoam ball head are good for beginners, too.

Actually, all the puppets given are easy to make; that's why they are in the book. The only one not recommended for young readers or people who are just beginning is the large two-hand puppet. Sewing the mouthpiece in place may be a little bit difficult the first time you do it, so wait till you have tried the easier designs before you try this one. But it is so much fun to work that it will be well worth whatever time and effort you put into it.

If you already have puppets which you made or which were manufactured, you can use them in your shows too. You can add costumes and props to make them become different characters.

There are many ways to make each of the characters in the three plays in Chapter 3. The designs and patterns are planned to help you learn a variety of ways to make puppets for future shows as well.

Only two kinds of puppets are really needed for "The Three Little Pigs" since all three pigs can be made with the same pattern and just dressed differently. I used the *small puppet body* pattern (see pages 70-71) with a $1\frac{3}{4}''$ styrofoam ball head for the first pig who wears just a collar and a bow tie. The second pig is made from the *easy half-circle puppet body* pattern (see page 74) with a head made from the toe of a sock. I dressed the second pig as a girl. The *small cloth puppet* pattern (see pages 60-61) was used for the third pig who wears blue felt overalls. Any one of these patterns can be used for all three pigs. Use different colors and clothing on each one. The wolf is made from a gray sock, as shown by the *sock puppet* directions (see page 59).

For "Little Red Riding Hood," granny was made from the large size circle shown on the directions for a *simple puppet from a circle of cloth* (see page 57). Red Riding Hood and the woodchopper are both made with the pattern for the *small puppet body*. She has a 3″ styrofoam ball head and the woodchopper has the same size head made from the toe of a sock. The wolf was made by the *talking puppet* directions (see page 58). Mother was made from the *easy half-circle puppet body* directions. You can use the same sock puppet wolf you used for "The Three Little Pigs" if you like.

Dewey was made by the same *talking puppet* directions as the wolf but he works just as well when made from a sock. The *small puppet body* pattern with a 3″ styrofoam ball head was used for Marian.

The lion and the mouse in the third play. "The Lion and the Mouse," work best if made by the patterns suggested because of their sizes and because of the parts they play. (The lion can, however, be made with the *large cloth puppet* pattern (see pages 62-63) if you are not ready to attempt the larger pattern yet.)

I made the lion of tan cloth and yarn with the *two-hand puppet* pattern (see pages 64-65) and the mouse of white cloth with the *miniature puppet body* pattern (see page 69). The mouse has a 1¾″ styrofoam ball head and I use a rod for the head movement.

Augustus was made from the *large puppet body* pattern (see pages 72-73) with a 3½″ styrofoam ball head. I used the *large cloth puppet* pattern for Disgustus. Both puppets are of pink cloth and both have black curly yarn hair.

The puppet bodies are sewn or glued completely from one side at the bottom, around the arms and neck and down the other side as indicated on the patterns. *No opening is left in the neck.* The puppeteer's finger fits inside the neck the same as it fits inside a glove finger. This makes glueing on the head easier and neater. The enclosed neck fits into the hole in the head and everything is positioned properly. There are no complicated necks to worry about, just turn the head so the face is in front, carefully remove your finger and stuff a little paper inside to hold everything in place while the glue dries. The paper is removed and a puppet is "born."

The steps are basically the same for all the patterns: trace the pattern from the book onto paper, use this pattern to pin onto the cloth, cut out the cloth puppet, glue or sew it, clip the curved seams, and turn it right side out.

If you label your patterns and glue a large envelope in the back of your book to store them in, you can use them over and over without having to trace them again.

Remember that no matter how beautiful a puppet is, people won't enjoy seeing it unless it is made to come alive in a creative way. Remember, too, that even the crudest puppet can be wonderfully interesting and funny when it is manipulated well. Making the puppet is only part of puppetry—you must give him his personality by the way you work him on stage.

chapter 5

Design Your Stage to Suit You and Your Budget

I'VE TRIED TO GIVE a variety of ideas for a stage so that no matter what age you are or how much money you have, you can find the stage best suited to you!

You may want to start with what things you have around the house, such as a table or curtain across a doorway or a table on its side. You can even work behind a chair or sofa. As with the puppets, a beautifully made stage is only a part of puppetry. A handsome, expensive one is not going to make your show a success. The only really important thing for a good show is that you be a good puppeteer, but you will eventually want a stage.

The simple stage made from a cardboard box is easy and requires no money at all. It is a good stage to start with.

My first ideas for a traveling stage were of metal or wood frames which strapped over my shoulders, but finally I realized that the easiest and most comfortable thing I could use was a plain corrugated cardboard box! What else would weigh so little, be so simple to construct, or so easy to find?

You can't easily give complete shows in the traveling stage because there is not much room between you and the stage opening. This stage is best suited for a particular kind of puppetry. When one strolls around at a school carnival or some other crowded place, the audience is moving, too! The best kind of show is the kind that you make up as you go along. You will find yourself talking to people who stop and talk to you. If your job is to stroll around and entertain, you might work out a very short skit to use with your conversations with people.

If your job is to advertise a puppet show or something else, you can make a sign with the information on it and fasten it to your traveling stage. By doing this, your job as strolling puppeteer will mostly be to answer questions about what you are advertising. People will ask the puppets, not you, so you will find the entertainment is in having the puppets talk to the people. It is particularly exciting for children to have the puppets speak directly to them.

The wood stage was designed to fit both children and grownups. Young children stand and the grownups and older children sit on chairs or stools. The stage folds so it can be taken places in a station wagon or in a car trunk. It can be folded and stored away when no one is using it. If you plan to travel about very much you can use one of those folding camp stools too.

There are so many ways to trim or decorate your stage that it would take pages to show even a few of them. You can trim it with real molding and pressed-wood decorations to make it look carved and elegant. Or you can paint it so that it looks as if it has carving and molding.

You can cover it with cloth or cut out designs from cloth and glue them on. You can glue on pictures or paint on any kind of design.

You can fasten on a small chalk board so that you can write titles or announcements on it, or you could fasten on a cork board and pin different signs to it. You can paint or cover it to match your own room or a den. You can paint on your Scout, club, church, or school emblem and colors.

PROPS AND SCENERY ARE FUN TO MAKE AND USE

Props, or properties, are objects other than the puppets which you use in your play, such as brooms, baskets, and so on. You will think of many clever props to add to your plays as you rehearse.

Put real flour or talcum powder in a prop broom or feather duster so that when the puppet sweeps or dusts there will be real "dust."

Confetti can be used for water, rain, or snow if you like. (Be prepared to sweep the floor after the show, though.) Various party and Halloween or New Year's noisemakers can be used for sound effects. Those party favors that uncurl when you blow them can be used for crazy tongues or for a puppet to really blow if you attach a tube to it.

A little metal "cricket" popper can actually be used in a puppet's mouth or for sound effects backstage. A cricket or a whistle can be used for a funny trick. A puppet can swallow it and you can make the sound from backstage.

Whistles and little horns can be used in the puppet's mouth. If you have another one to blow backstage, it will appear as though he is really blowing it. You can make a drum out of a can or oatmeal box and glue or sew drumsticks to a puppet's hands so he can really beat it.

The play "The Three Little Pigs" requires the three houses of straw, sticks, and bricks. The directions for making these of cardboard are on the "props" pages. If you give the play alone, the pins on the back of the houses will free your hand so that you can work the wolf. When someone helps you, the pins can be closed and not used. With one person working with you, one of you can manipulate all three pigs and the other one the wolf. Three or four people can do the play with each person manipulating one puppet, but it is written so that you can do it by yourself if you prefer. The feather duster and the broom are described on the "props" pages also.

For "Little Red Riding Hood" you will need Dewey's book, a basket of goodies, and the woodchopper's club. If you like, you can add a broom for Mother and a flower for the forest scene and perhaps a bottle of medicine or a handkerchief for Granny.

The props required for "The Lion and the Mouse" are a net or a rope and a spear for Disgustus. You could add a bee on a wire for the sleeping scene. You could even have the lion use a comb and a mirror for grooming or a pillow for his head to rest on when he sleeps. This scene is so full of possibilities that you can even go as far as having him cover himself with a blanket and wear a nightcap or a crown on his head.

Often props become *visual jokes* because either the prop itself or the manner in which it is used by the puppet makes the audience laugh. Usually these visual jokes can be added to a play without a single change in the dialogue.

SCENERY, BACK CURTAINS AND LIGHTS

With props you can make your audience imagine that the puppets are in a house or a forest, but if you prefer to have a scene in back of your puppets, it is easy to make one. Just draw and color the scene on cloth with crayons.

The back curtain should come just an inch or so below the stage opening so that it covers the opening but leaves space to get your arms underneath. Either hem the top or use clip-on curtain rings to hang the curtain on the rod. With the clip-on rings there is no need to sew anything at all. Hang your curtain and go sit in front of the stage to check where the scene should go, and mark it. The scene will be larger than the stage opening because the audience can see back into the stage. After you mark it, draw the design in with a light-colored crayon such as white, gray, or yellow. Then color the fireplace, trees, or whatever you have drawn, by pressing fairly hard with the crayons to make the colors bright. After you finish, you can iron the scene over paper and the crayon will melt and become brighter. It can even be laundered and it won't wash out! This method is so neat, so easy and inexpensive, that you will want to use it for all your scenes.

The best place to get ideas for this back curtain is from story books, perhaps the same book where you got the story for your play. You can add other details to the scenes to make them exciting, such as glitter or beads to a chandelier. You can hang window curtains or dollhouse pictures onto your room scenes. If you want a wallpaper design for your room, just use flowered or figured cloth and glue on pictures, windows, or doors from other cloth or cardboard.

You can use an inexpensive unbleached muslin or cotton cloth or old table cloths, sheets, or full-skirted dresses. You can use colored cloth if you like, such

Use an inexpensive cotton cloth or an old sheet for the back curtains for your stage. Draw and color the scene with crayon. Use clip-on curtain rings to hold the curtain on the rod. You can use as many as three scenes on the rod at one time and slide them across the rod as needed during the show. Leave the bottom edge plain or sew or glue in a hem. When not in use, these scenes can be folded and stored in a drawer.

as a light green or tan on which to draw and color a forest scene, or a blue, perhaps, for an indoor scene. The least expensive cotton cloth is the best for back curtains because it is thin enough so that you can see through it when your stage light is on.

When you change scenes with the cloth curtains, slide the curtain rings so that one scene is shifted all the way to one side while the new one is spread out in place. You can plan for as many as three scenes this way if you need them. You simply reach up and slide them from behind and the audience doesn't even see what moves them. The scenes should be pinned or clipped together so they all slide, one after the other.

I have never, in all the years of my work with puppets, found a better or less expensive stage light than an ordinary bed lamp. If it doesn't fit exactly, just bend the metal clamps so that they do fit. You can use it on top shining down or on the bottom of the stage shining up. (See sketch on pattern page.)

The stage can be folded, the cloth scenes folded with the curtain rings still clipped on, and the light removed and everything stored away easily this way.

THE SCRIPT

Since the puppeteer is backstage and it's the puppet who is seen by the audience, you don't have to memorize your lines if you can manage to read them. After several rehearsals you won't need to read every word but only glance at the script every now and then to see what you say next.

How are you going to hold the script when your hands are busy working the puppets? If the script were only one page, you could tape it somewhere on the

Pin or staple your script pages together. Keep another pin in the corner for fastening the script to your lap. You can flip the pages easily and quickly and your script won't slide off your lap this way.

You won't actually read your script during the play if you rehearse it several times. The script just gives you confidence. You can glance down at it every now and then. This way you can concentrate on manipulating your puppets.

inside of the stage and that would be simple enough, but most plays will take up several pages.

My own children, my students, and I find the best way after writing out the script is to underline certain characters' names with certain colors. For instance, Red Riding Hood's name could be underlined each time in red throughout the play. The puppeteer who works her can quickly and easily spot her lines at a glance.

We then take a straight pin or safety pin and pin the script pages together at one of the top corners as shown in the drawing. (A paper clip will not work because it will slip and come loose.) Then we take another pin and pin the script onto our lap to our clothing as shown in the drawing, to prevent it from falling off during the play. We put this pin close to the pin which holds the pages together. You can turn the pages easily and quickly this way and you need only glance down to see your lines.

We tried everything from hanging the script on the curtains to attaching it to the inside of the stage but we have found this is the easiest and best method for us. If you fasten the script to the curtain or stage, there is no way to turn the pages. A clipboard or notebook can be used on your lap but sometimes it may fall off during the play.

When you copy your script to use during your play it isn't necessary to copy all the directions. Just copy the dialogue which the puppets speak; you will remember to act out the movements you planned when you rehearsed the show.

chapter **6**

Learn to Make Your Puppets "Come Alive"

ALWAYS REMEMBER THAT if you are going to perform before an audience as small as even one or two people, you owe it to them to entertain them to the best of your ability. Your best as far as puppetry is concerned means how well you can make your puppet *perform* while he talks. Remember that your puppet can have only as much life as you can give him. Without a puppeteer he is nothing; with a good puppeteer he is many things!

If you play with your puppets for years and practice with them, you will learn to make them do more than you now dream they can do, but why spend years learning some of the simple movements which I can show you in a few moments? Think of this book as giving you a head start toward becoming a good puppeteer.

The exercises and positions are just the beginning. The more you practice them, the more you will learn, and the better a puppeteer you will be. After you think you have learned them, it is a good idea to go through them again each time before you give a show, just as a singer goes through voice exercises or a skater does warming-up exercises.

FINGER EXERCISES

Let's make sure you know which fingers I mean when I say *index* finger or second finger. The drawing of the hand shows what puppeteers call each finger.

The up-and-down line is a *vertical* line. When a puppet is vertical he is upright as if he were standing very straight. The line going across from side to side is a *horizontal* line. When a puppet is horizontal he is lying down. When his arms are horizontal they are straight out from his sides. The line where the sky and

41

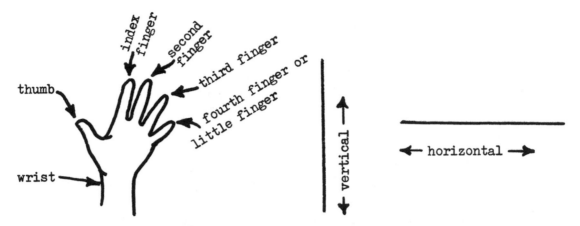

the ground meet is the horizon; remember, then, that horizontal is going the way the horizon goes. A person is vertical when he stands. The floor or ground he stands on is horizontal.

1.   2.   3.   4.

It's our hands that make a hand puppet move. Now let's do a simple exercise *without* a puppet so we know what our hands do when they are inside a puppet.

A. 1.   Hold your hand in an upright, or vertical, position.
      2.   Hold your index finger pointing straight up and fold all your other fingers down. Put your thumb over the folded fingers as in picture 2. Your index finger goes into the puppet's head.
      3.   Keep holding your index finger straight up and hold your thumb and second finger out as far as you can, as in picture 3, keeping your third and fourth fingers still folded. If you had a puppet on your hand now, your index finger would be in the head and your thumb and second finger would be in the arms.
      4.   Sometimes you can use your thumb in one arm and your second, third, and fourth fingers all in the other arm as in picture 4. (The puppets which have holes cut so your fingers become their arms must be manipulated or worked with your third and fourth fingers folded as in picture 3.)

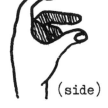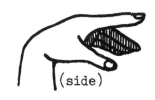

1.　　　　　　　　　　　　　　　　2.

B. 1. Next, hold your hand as though you have a puppet on it, as you did in exercise A. Bend just your index finger joint, as in picture 1. This will make a puppet nod his head. Raise your finger now so that it is vertical again.

   2. This time, keep your index finger joint *straight* and bend your wrist only, as in picture 2. This will make your puppet bend over at the hips if he is a small puppet or at the waist if he is large. The finger and the wrist movements are two individual movements.

That's enough with your bare hand. Let's try it with a puppet; it's more fun! Remember, you will be behind your puppet so when he faces front he has his back to you. Your audience will be in front of you and in front of your puppet. Don't get in the habit of having your puppet face *you;* then he would have his back to the audience. *The drawings show the way the audience sees him.*

It will help if someone else will read the directions to you while you manipulate the puppets. This person can tell you if you are doing it correctly. The back of the puppet is shaded in the drawings to help you see at a glance which way he is turned.

Get behind a stage, a sofa, chair, table, or something else so that you are out of sight and only your puppet is seen.

If you do the exercises alone, try doing them in front of a mirror. You should get down low or to one side so that you see only your puppet and not yourself in the mirror.

Whether you work behind a stage or with a mirror you should hold your puppet high enough to be seen, but not so high that the bottom of the puppet body-dress can be seen. Hand puppets don't have legs so you must keep that part of his body below the edge of the stage; the audience will imagine that he has legs.

BASIC HAND PUPPET MOVEMENTS

C. 1. When you have your puppet placed with his head on your index finger and his arms on your thumb and second finger (or all your other fingers), make him face one side, as shown in picture 1.

   2. Now turn him to face the audience. Keep him upright, or vertical, as in

1.   2.   3.   4.

picture 2. Remember that the picture shows the puppet the way the audience sees him.

3. Turn him to face the other side, still keeping him vertical, as in picture 3.

4. Turn him around to face you so that his back is to the audience as in picture 4. It is easy to turn a puppet to face the back when you turn him toward your body. When you turn him away from you, you have to twist your hand around. Practice both directions so that you will learn to make your puppet face in any direction.

5. Put him on your other hand and do the same thing. You should learn to work your puppets as easily with one hand as with the other whether you are right- or left-handed.

1.   2.   3.   4.

D. 1. Nod just your puppet's head toward one side as shown in the drawing. Bend your index finger only. Keep his body upright, or vertical, and his hands out, or horizontal.

2. Have him face the audience and nod his head, keeping his body upright.

3. Turn him to the other side and have him nod his head, then straighten up.

4. Turn him around so that his back is to the audience and have him nod once more, then straighten up.

44

5. Put him on your other hand and repeat the whole exercise, remembering to bend only your index finger and not your wrist.

1.   2.   3.   4.

E. 1. This time, bend your wrist so that the puppet bows from his hips. (If you use a large puppet he will bend at his waist.) Make him face one side and bend over, then straighten up. Keep his arms out in a horizontal position.
    2. Make him face the audience, bend over, then straighten up.
    3. Make him turn to the other side, bend over, as in picture 3, then straighten up.
    4. Turn him all the way around till his back is to the audience, bend him over as in picture 4, then straighten him up.
    5. Put the puppet on your other hand and repeat, following the pictures. Keep your fingers straight and bend just your wrist.

1.   2.

Now for the real fun!

F. 1. Move your puppet in from one side until he reaches the middle of your stage. Make him stop for a moment and then look down as he did in exercise D. Pretend he sees something on the floor which he doesn't understand. Make him bend over, as he did in exercise E, to get a better look or to pick it up. Be sure that you keep this two different movements. First he looks down, then he bends over, as in picture 1.
    2. Turn him to face the audience, have him nod just his head to look down. Keep his body upright, or vertical. Then have him bend over as before. Straighten him up.

3.

4.

3. Turn him to the other side, have him look down, bend over, then straighten up.
4. Turn him so that his back is to the audience, make him look down, then bend over. Straighten him up, have him turn to the side and move across the stage.
5. Put him on your other hand and repeat the exercise.

You have now learned the basic puppet positions. He can face front, either side, and back. His neck bends and his waist or hips can bend.

But what about his arms? He has been holding them straight out all this time, hasn't he? Let's practice a few arm movements and see some of the things he can do. When the puppet faces the audience, he has his back to you so *his* right is on *your* right and *his* left is on *your* left. That's easy enough to remember, isn't it? (If you just made your puppet nod his head "yes" to that question—good for you!)

1.   2.   3.   4.   5.   6.

G. 1. Have your puppet face the audience with his arms straight out to the side in a horizontal position.
2. Have him put his left hand on his stomach while his right arm is still straight out. Straighten his arm.
3. Put his right hand on his stomach, then back in the straight-out position while his left arm stays out straight.
4. Now have him put both hands on his stomach.
5. Now have him put his hands together out in front of him. Have him clap his hands.
6. Have him put his right hand on his stomach and bow to the audience.

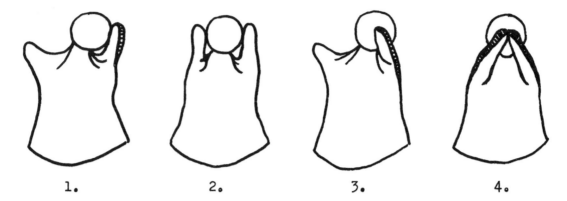

1.   2.   3.   4.

H.   1.   Make him touch his ear with his left hand, then with his right.
     2.   Place both hands over his ears as though he doesn't want to hear some-thing. Nod his head when you do this so his hands reach his ears.
     3.   Put his left hand on his nose, then his right hand on his nose.
     4.   Have him cover his face with both hands. Make him cry. Make him cover his face because he is frightened, then slowly raise his head and remove his hands to see if the coast is clear. Make him rub his eyes because he is sleepy. Have him cover a yawn. Make him brush his hair back, rub his nose, his ear, and scratch his head. Have him put *one* hand on his stomach and the other under his chin as though thinking. How many other things can you make him do?

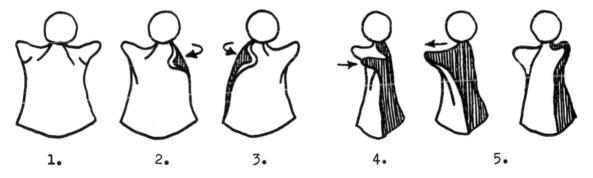

1.   2.   3.   4.   5.

Now for something a little harder!

I.   1.   Start with his arms straight out, or horizontal, and his body upright, or vertical, as in picture 1.
     2.   Swing his whole left arm around so that he points straight ahead. Straighten it back out to the side.
     3.   Swing his right arm around and point straight ahead. Put it back out to the side.
     4.   Now, see if you can pull his left arm back as though it is bent at his elbow, if he had one, as in picture 4. This is like a boxer pulling back

getting ready to sock someone. You have to bend your finger and thumb at your knuckle for this.

5. Now, push his hand straight out as though to punch someone or to push something away! Do one of his hands, then the other, as though boxing. If you do this over and over, he will appear to be swimming. Have him pretend to hand someone something. Make him reach out and pretend to take something someone is giving him. Make him point to someone as though to say, "He did it!" Make him throw a kiss to the audience with his left hand, then his right, then with both hands. What else can you make him do using this push-pull movement?

Have you noticed that your arm and hand muscles are getting tired? You are using muscles you don't often use. If you practice with your puppet, your muscles will get stronger and you will be able to do all these exercises better. If your arms are good and tired you get an "A"; it means you've been working!

Did you know that the way a person or animal walks tells us much about him? An elephant sways from side to side, a duck waddles, a rabbit hops, a turtle moves slowly, and a squirrel leaps and bounces quickly across the yard. An old person leans forward when he walks, and a princess holds her head high and her body straight. Some people bounce up and down when they walk, some sway from side to side, and some rock back and forth.

We are going to make a puppet walk, a puppet who doesn't even have legs or feet! The audience will have to *imagine* that he walks, runs, or jumps because of the way *you* move him. If you do it well they will even think they *see* him do it! Remember, the better a puppeteer you are, the more the audience will imagine.

up and down   twisting   back and forth   side-to-
bobbing movement   movement   rocking movement   side sway

J. Your puppet must do things in miniature because a small cardboard stage opening may be only about 14 to 18 inches wide and even a larger wood stage may be only a little over 2 feet wide. If you want him to appear to walk halfway across the stage, you are going to have to have a number of move-

48

ments in a small space. Have you ever "marked time" or marched while standing in the same spot without going anywhere? If you haven't, try it now. A puppet must often walk in almost this way—he may travel only an inch or so with each step so that he *appears* to be going some place fast while actually he is "marking time."

UP-AND-DOWN BOBBING MOVEMENTS

1. Each time, bring your puppet from the side. Have him turn to the back and go for a distance with his back to the audience. Make him stop, turn around, and go back toward the audience. Now, have him turn and continue across the stage.

    The first time have him do this with a very short up-and-down bobbing movement. A little mouse and a young girl would walk this way, wouldn't they?
2. Have him go the same way, only this time with an up-and-over movement more like hopping or leaping. This will be almost like drawing circles in the air.
3. Make him bob up and down very fast as though running from a bad wolf!
4. Make him move up and down slowly as though he has been running a long distance and is worn out. (I hope you instinctively made him mop his brow just then.)
5. How many animals can you make him be? What about a kangaroo? a bunny? a small dog?

TWISTING AROUND-AND-BACK MOVEMENTS

1. Move your puppet across the stage as before, only this time twist your wrist around and then back as you go. He really appears to be taking steps, doesn't he?
2. Do this again with very small, fast, twisting movements.
3. Do it with large, slow twists.
4. Now try large but fast twists. This appears to be a frantic run! If your puppet has long hair, the hair will fly and flip and add to the frantic look.
5. This time try small and slow twists. This is a dainty princess-like walk, isn't it?
6. What else can you think of to add to this twisting around-and-back movement? This is a good movement for a girl puppet in a full skirt or cape because the twisting will make the skirt move.

BACK-AND-FORTH ROCKING MOVEMENT

1. This time as the puppet walks, have him rock forward, then backward, then forward, then backward, and so on, as he goes.
2. Do this quickly so he appears to take very small, quick steps.

3. Do it again with large slow back-and-forth movements; it looks as though he is taking large steps.

4. Move him up and down at the same time he goes back and forth with an up-and-over walk.

5. Lean him forward as he rocks like an old, old person. Lean him backward with a "stuck-up" kind of walk. Now have him look at the ground as though looking for something. Have him look at the sky, at a bird, or airplane, or witch as he walks. This would be a natural place for him to stub his toe and fall or run into something, wouldn't it?

6. Can you make him lose his balance and almost fall? Can you make him walk as though he has the hiccups?

SIDE-TO-SIDE SWAYING MOVEMENT

1. Hold the puppet standing upright, or vertical, and lean him first to his left, then to his right. Don't make him go forward or back, just from one side to the other. Take him across the stage on his trip as before.

2. Do this side-to-side sway with large movements so that he leans way over each time. Do it slowly. Do it fast.

3. Use very small, side-to-side swaying this time. Do it slowly. Do it again quickly so that it is a nervous kind of walk.

4. Move the puppet up and down as he sways from side to side. This makes an up-and-over movement, doesn't it? This gives the impression of a limp, perhaps like the walk of a pirate with a wooden leg or an animal or person with a hurt foot.

5. Can you think of other ways to use this movement to make a person or animal seem large or small, relaxed or nervous, and even kind or mean?

Now that you have learned most of the basic puppet movements you can begin to combine them. Use one of the arm movements at the same time you use one of the walking movements. He can push and pull with his arms or swing them from side to side while he rocks back and forth. He can bring his arms together over his stomach and then back out to his side or he can bring one in front and then the other one.

He can bend his body or nod his head as he sways from side to side. There are so many possibilities that you must now be left on your own to experiment with all I've told you. You can, with practice, make your puppet appear to swim, fly, skip, slink, slither, hop, gallop, crawl, and so on and on!

ROD PUPPETS

Almost any puppet can have a rod glued into it to give it still other movements. Use a new pencil, "tinkertoy" stick, a paper tube from a coat hanger, or a wood dowel for a rod.

1. Hold the rod as shown in Diagram 1. A puppet can shake his head "no" or

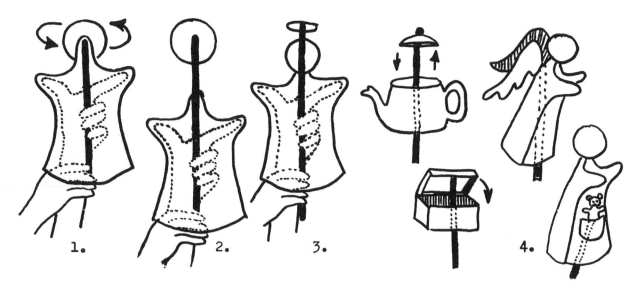

1.　　　2.　　　3.　　　4.

look behind him. He can look, turn away and look back quickly for a "double take," which is always funny. He can turn his head all the way around while looking at an insect or have his head twist all the way around because someone slaps him.

He can keep looking behind him as he walks or runs. He can turn his back to the audience and then turn his head to look at them over his shoulder.

His head can move up and down. He can shrug his shoulders. He can touch the top of his head with his hands when the rod is pulled to make his head move down. His head can move up and down as his body stays still or moves from side to side. If he is a turtle he can pull his head into his shell!

2. The head can be separate from the body so it can go up into the air as in Diagram 2. This can be used for some wild fight scenes or for scary scenes.

3. The rod can go all the way through the head and be attached to a hat, horns, or a halo which will turn, bounce, or act in its own way as in Diagram 3. The puppet could even be a teapot which blows its top or a box which opens itself!

4. The rod can come out the back and operate a tail or wings or a papoose as in Diagram 4. Or it can come out the front for a baby kangaroo in his mother's pouch or something in a pocket. It can even be on the outside for controlling a hand or tail.

TALKING PUPPETS

A talking puppet can do much more than just open and close his mouth. This puppet, whether made from a sock or some other material, can be made to smile or frown by the way you move your fingers.

If you fold your fingers over your thumb you can get some funny expressions. You can open his mouth so wide that his tongue will appear to move out. With the right sounds he can spit, sputter, stick out his tongue, cough, sneeze, bite his lip, lick his lips, and so on.

One of the best ways to practice is first to see how many things you can make your own mouth do and then see if you can make your puppet do them too. Try this in front of a mirror. The more you experiment the more you will learn to do, and the funnier your puppet will be!

TWO-HAND PUPPETS

There really aren't any rules to learn for this puppet because when you use both your hands to work him you can make him do almost anything you want him to do. The pattern can be used for people or animal puppets and the movements are real enough to convince very young audiences that the puppet is really alive!

You must first learn how to place your hands inside him. You can use either of your hands in his head. If you use your left hand in his head, then you put your right hand in his right hand. Then, of course, if you use your right hand for his head and mouth, your left hand manipulates his left hand. You are behind him. You work his mouth the same way you work the sock puppet's mouth. You will need to get the cotton stuffed in the head so that your hand goes right to the mouth and the head stays upright. The cotton should rest on the top of your fingers. When you get his head so that you can work his mouth comfortably there's no end to what you can make him do!

You can make him rub his eyes, or scratch his nose, his head, his chin, or his ears. He can arrange his hair, put on or take off a hat, suck his thumb, or bite his nails! He can yawn, lick his paw, rub his stomach, feed himself, drink from a cup, comb his own hair, look into a hand mirror, and even fasten his own clothes and many, many other things. Just practice in front of a mirror till you know how the movements look to the audience as well as how they feel to your hands inside the puppet. Eventually you will be able to switch hands inside this puppet so that he can use both his hands during a performance.

A puppet not only can do what we can, but he can do *more* than we ever could! Can we take off our head and then put it back on? Can we fly? Can we die and come back to life? Can we blow a house away or chew a rope in two? Can a worm read or a wolf wear clothes and talk? If he is a puppet, he can do all these things and much, much more.

Now you must begin to look around you and observe what people and animals do and then think about how you can make your puppets act like them. I can give you a few simple rules for making a puppet open his mouth or run, but there is much more to puppetry and to life than that. You must now begin to make a puppet open his mouth in a certain way—to show astonishment, fright, or greed. You must make him run like an evil wolf, walk like a beautiful princess, or scramble like a frightened pig. In other words, it's *how* you make him do things that gives him character.

From now on, the kind of puppeteer you become will depend on what you do with all you have learned about puppetry.

Patterns for Puppets

TOOLS AND MATERIALS

PUPPET BODIES

HEADS, FACES
   AND HAIR

COSTUMES

PROPS AND STAGES

TOOLS AND MATERIALS

scissors for cutting any of the materials used.

kitchen knife for cutting corrugated cardboard used for stages.

white liquid glue in a dispenser bottle for puppets, costumes, and props. This same glue is used in larger quantities for making the stages.

styrofoam balls various sizes for puppet heads and features. They are used for some props also.

pins to hold patterns on cloth while cutting and to hold features and trim in place while glue dries.

needle and thread for any sewing you want to do on the puppets and costumes.

cloth for puppet bodies in any color to represent the skin color you want. Other colors and prints for puppet clothes and for stage curtains.

paper either tissue, wax paper, or white wrapping or drawing paper for tracing the patterns for puppets and puppet bodies and clothes.

yarn for puppet hair, animal manes, tails, etc., and for some props.

fur, fringe, pompon fringe, lace, braid, feathers, ribbon, rickrack, etc. for puppet hair and for trim and props.

cotton for stuffing puppet heads or hands. Also for puppet hair, whiskers.

paper tubes from coathangers for rods for puppets and props. Other rods such as "tinkertoy" sticks, pencils, and dowels can be used.

cardboard any type for making props.

old socks for making sock puppets.

old shirt sleeves for shirt-sleeve puppets.

old jewelery, beads, buttons, sequins for eyes, noses, trims and other things.

felt scraps to be used for features on faces and trim on costumes.

old stockings to cover styrofoam ball heads and for stuffing and puppet hair.

large corrugated cardboard boxes for box stage and for traveling stage.

small boxes for props, and for holding props and odds and ends.

small toys for props such as dishes, baskets, play food, dollhouse pictures and so on.

pencil for tracing patterns and for marking and drawing props and puppets.

crayons for drawing and coloring scenery, curtains, and for puppets and costumes.

safety pins (small) for attaching props to curtains (see props pages) and for puppet clothes.

materials for wood stage are listed on the directions page for the wood stage.

curtain rod for hanging the back curtain. Rods such as a yardstick, a broomstick, or a dowel can be used also.

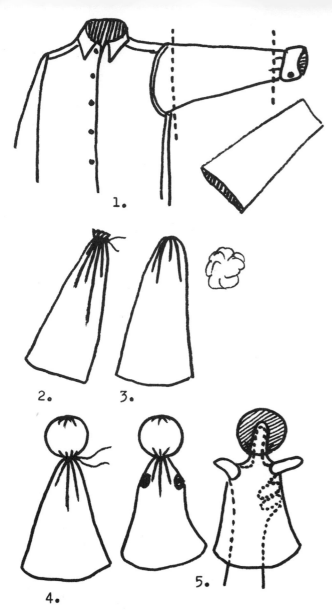

AN OLD SHIRT SLEEVE CAN BECOME A PUPPET!

1. Use the sleeve of an old shirt or blouse. Cut it as shown in step 1 and turn it inside out.
2. Tie a string around one end **very tightly**, as shown in step 2.
3. Turn it right side out.
4. Stuff cotton, facial tissue, paper towels, or some other stuffing in the head and tie another string around the neck. Leave room for your finger to go up into the head, inside the stuffing.
5. Place your index finger way up into the head, then cut small holes for your thumb and second finger as shown in step 5.
6. Glue on the face and hair.

Make a hat, a collar, and a belt for a woodchopper, or a nightcap for a grandmother.

A red cape and hood will make this puppet a Red Riding Hood.

Add a button nose, some felt ears, and eyes, and you have a pig.

This simple little puppet can be many characters for many plays and not a bit of sewing is necessary!

2.

3.

4.

5.

6.

MAKE A SIMPLE PUPPET FROM A CIRCLE OF CLOTH

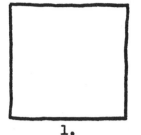

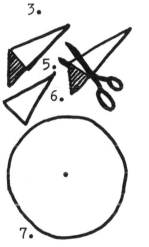

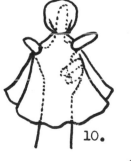

1. Use a 30-inch square of cloth to make a large puppet, a 24-inch square for a small puppet and one 15 inches square for a miniature puppet.
2. Fold the square in half.
3. Fold it again as in step 3. Mark the center with a dot.
4. Fold it again to make a triangle.
5. And fold it once more as in step 5.
6. Cut with scissors so the edges are all even.
7. Unfold it and you have a circle with the center marked.
8. Take a wad of cotton or some other kind of stuffing such as facial tissue, old stockings, foam rubber, kapok or bits of cloth and place it in the center.
9. Fold the circle of cloth around the stuffing and place a rubber band around it or tie a string around it so that you have a head. Leave enough room for your finger to go inside the head.
10. Work a hole up into the stuffing for your index finger. Cut two small holes where your thumb and second finger come, and you have a basic puppet ready for a face and hair.
11. You can glue in a rod such as a pencil, a paper tube from a coathanger, a "tinkertoy" stick or something similar and you have a hand-and-rod puppet.

This type of puppet is well suited for girl characters such as Little Red Riding Hood and Grandmother.

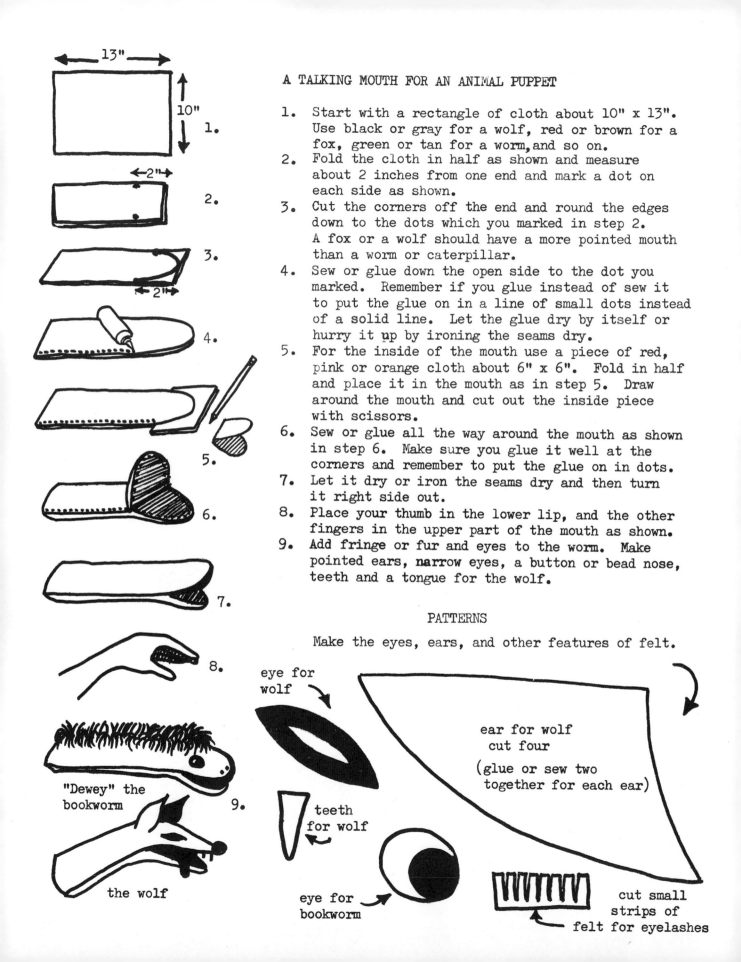

A TALKING MOUTH FOR AN ANIMAL PUPPET

1. Start with a rectangle of cloth about 10" x 13". Use black or gray for a wolf, red or brown for a fox, green or tan for a worm, and so on.

2. Fold the cloth in half as shown and measure about 2 inches from one end and mark a dot on each side as shown.

3. Cut the corners off the end and round the edges down to the dots which you marked in step 2. A fox or a wolf should have a more pointed mouth than a worm or caterpillar.

4. Sew or glue down the open side to the dot you marked. Remember if you glue instead of sew it to put the glue on in a line of small dots instead of a solid line. Let the glue dry by itself or hurry it up by ironing the seams dry.

5. For the inside of the mouth use a piece of red, pink or orange cloth about 6" x 6". Fold in half and place it in the mouth as in step 5. Draw around the mouth and cut out the inside piece with scissors.

6. Sew or glue all the way around the mouth as shown in step 6. Make sure you glue it well at the corners and remember to put the glue on in dots.

7. Let it dry or iron the seams dry and then turn it right side out.

8. Place your thumb in the lower lip, and the other fingers in the upper part of the mouth as shown.

9. Add fringe or fur and eyes to the worm. Make pointed ears, narrow eyes, a button or bead nose, teeth and a tongue for the wolf.

PATTERNS

Make the eyes, ears, and other features of felt.

eye for wolf

ear for wolf
cut four

(glue or sew two together for each ear)

teeth for wolf

"Dewey" the bookworm

the wolf

eye for bookworm

cut small strips of felt for eyelashes

1. Use an old sock. Wool or fleecy socks work best but any will do.
2. Spread the sock out flat so that the heel is on top as in step 2. The sock should be wrong side out.
3. Cut around the edge of the toe and back about 2" or 3" as shown.
4. You will need a small piece of red, pink or orange cloth folded in half as shown. Put the folded cloth inside the open part of the mouth so that the folded edge fits all the way back against the end of the cut. Draw around the mouth as shown with pencil or chalk. Remove the cloth and cut out the mouthpiece.
5. Sew or glue it into the sock as in step 5.
6. Turn the sock right side out when the glue is dry or the seam has been ironed dry.
7. The thumb should work the bottom lip while all the fingers work the upper lip.
8. Glue or sew on features for faces. Stuff a little cotton into the heel to give the head shape.

You can be so creative with this easy-to-make puppet that you will think of many more animals and "creatures" to make!

1.
2.
3.
4.
5.
6.
7.

the wolf

8.

"Dewey" the bookworm

turtle   snake

a chicken, duck or goose

all kinds of dogs

horses or cows

reindeer

59

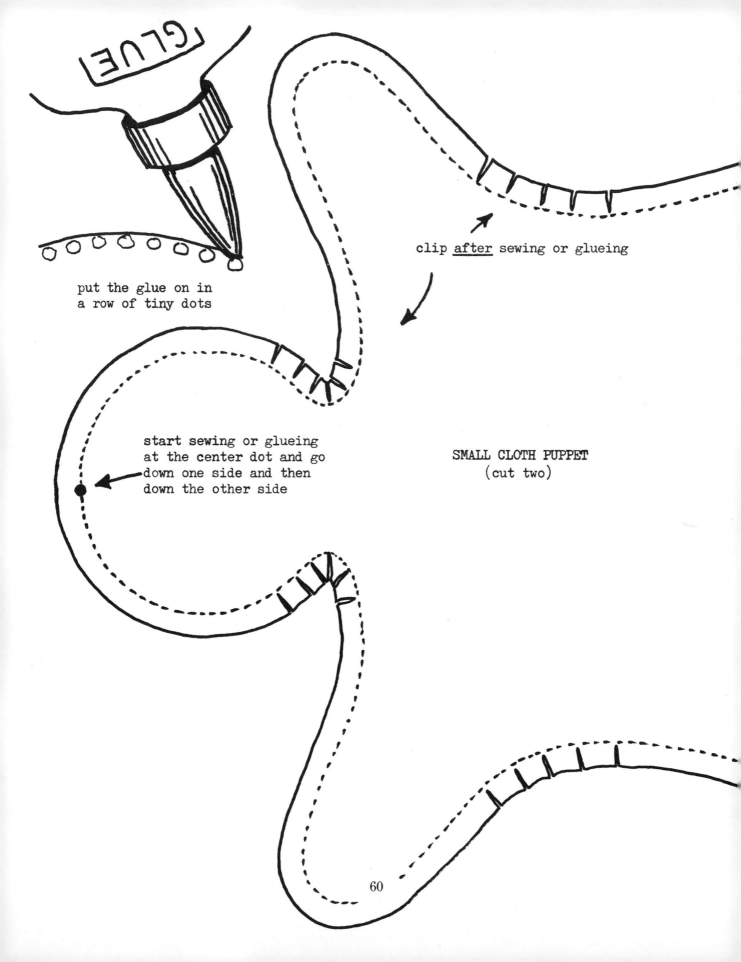

GLUE

put the glue on in
a row of tiny dots

clip _after_ sewing or glueing

start sewing or glueing
at the center dot and go
down one side and then
down the other side

SMALL CLOTH PUPPET
(cut two)

60

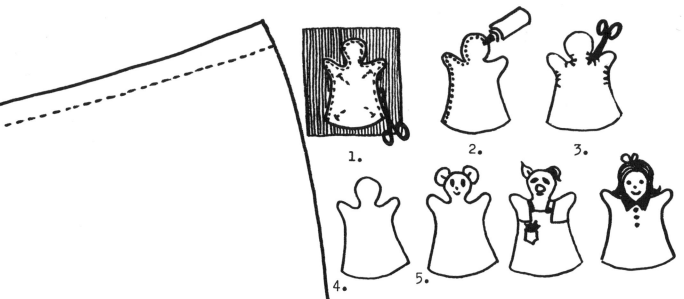

1.

2.

3.

4.

5.

SMALL CLOTH PUPPET

1. Trace the pattern onto tissue or wax paper. Mark the clips and the center dot. Place your pattern on two thicknesses of cloth and cut with scissors.
2. Sew or glue from the center dot at the top of the head and go down one side, and then down the other. Let dry.
3. Clip with your scissors point at the places shown on the pattern.
4. Turn right side out and stuff head with cotton or some other stuffing. Leave a hole in the cotton for your finger to go up into.
5. Glue on the face and hair for whatever character you want. This puppet can be almost any character you want to make.

This puppet works well with just your fingers or as a hand-and-rod puppet.

glue or sew where dotted lines are on the pattern

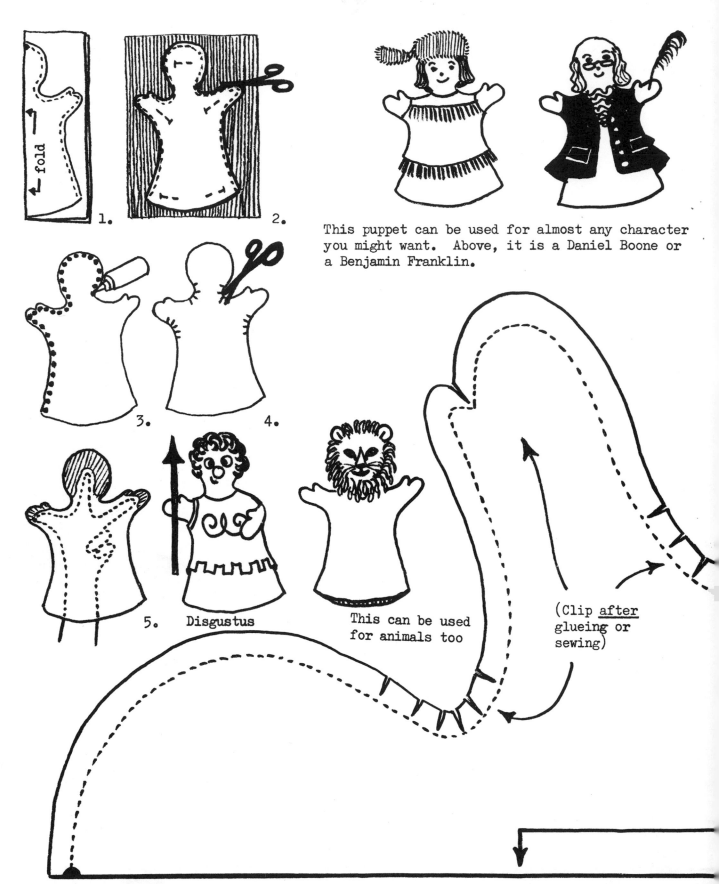

1.

2.

This puppet can be used for almost any character you might want. Above, it is a Daniel Boone or a Benjamin Franklin.

3.

4.

5.   Disgustus

This can be used for animals too

(Clip after glueing or sewing)

LARGE CLOTH PUPPET

1. Trace the pattern onto a piece of folded tissue or wax paper. Place the
   straight side of the pattern on the folded edge so that you will have a whole
   pattern after you cut it out.
2. Place your pattern on your cloth and cut two whole puppet pieces at one time.
   (Do not cut the clips until after the puppet body is glued or sewn together.)
3. Glue or sew where the dotted lines are on the pattern. If you glue the pieces
   together, put the glue on in small dots close to the edge, as shown. You can
   iron the seam dry in a few minutes if you want to. Start your sewing or
   glueing at the top of the head and go down one side to the bottom and then
   down the other side.
4. Clip with your scissors at the places shown on the patterns so the puppet can
   be turned right side out.
5. Stuff the head and hands with cotton or some other stuffing. Make or
   leave a hole going up into the head stuffing for your finger.
   Glue on hair, ears, and features for the character you want.

You can make this puppet out of knit cotton cloth such as an old undershirt or
T-shirt. You can make the face like the ones described on the page titled
CREATE MANY FACES WITH SOCK HEADS. You will need to tie a string around the
neck or stitch around it because the knit cloth is stretchy.

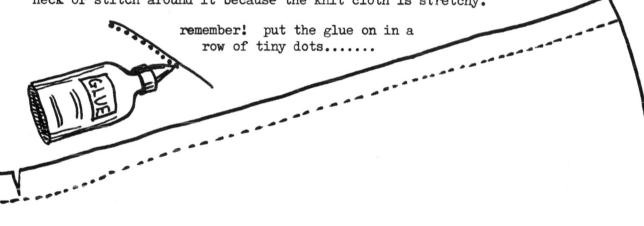

remember! put the glue on in a
row of tiny dots.......

LARGE CLOTH PUPPET

(This is only half the pattern. Cut two whole pieces
from cloth.)

place this line on the fold

You should have made several of the
smaller puppets before you try
this one.

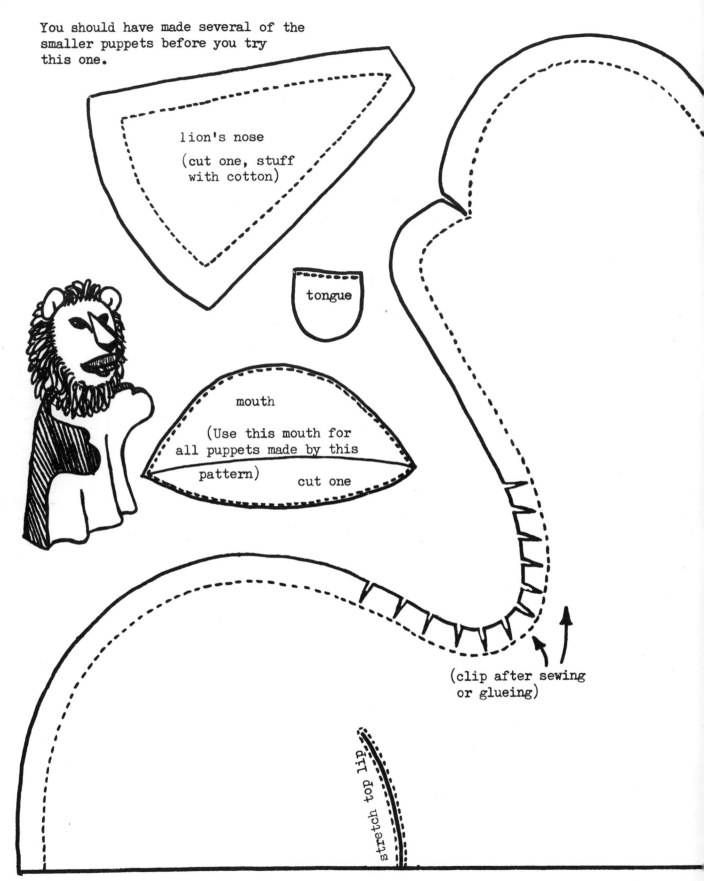

lion's nose

(cut one, stuff
with cotton)

tongue

mouth

(Use this mouth for
all puppets made by this
pattern)   cut one

(clip after sewing
or glueing)

stretch top lip

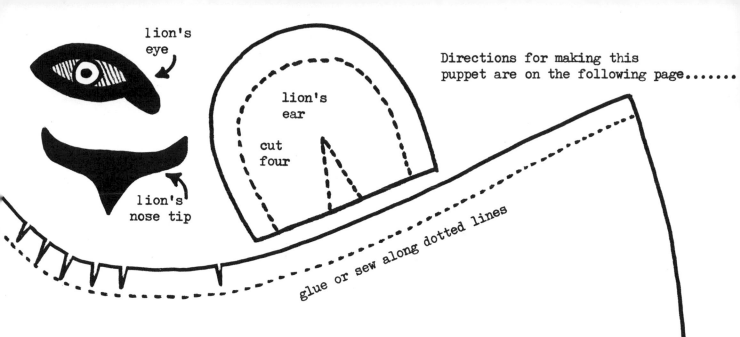

lion's
eye

lion's
nose tip

lion's
ear

cut
four

Directions for making this
puppet are on the following page.......

glue or sew along dotted lines

TWO-HAND PUPPET

(This is only half the
pattern. Place the
straight edge on the
fold when you cut your
paper pattern.)

place this edge on the fold to make a whole pattern

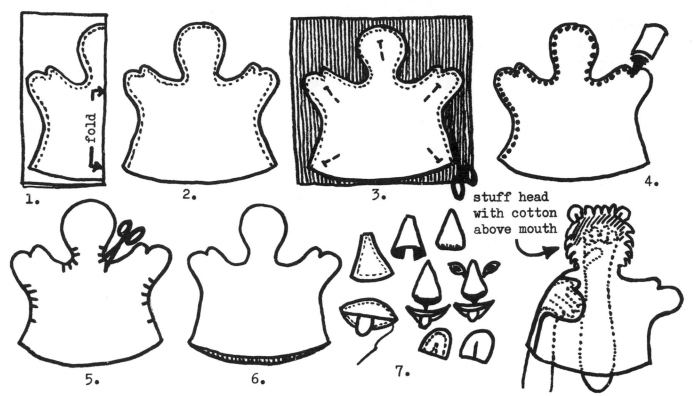

stuff head
with cotton
above mouth

1. 2. 3. 4. 5. 6. 7.

Put your left hand in his
head and your right hand
in his right hand

TWO-HAND PUPPET

1. Trace the pattern on a folded piece of tissue or wax paper. Place the straight
   edge of the pattern on the folded edge of the paper as shown in step 1. Be sure
   to trace the seam lines, nose and mouth on your pattern.
2. Cut it out, unfold it and you have a whole pattern as in step 2.
3. Place your pattern on two thicknesses of cloth and cut around it.
4. Glue or sew where the dotted lines are on the pattern. This puppet works
   better if it is sewn but it can be glued if done carefully.
5. Clip with your scissors point where clips are on the pattern. The clipping is
   important because the puppet won't turn right side out properly unless it is
   clipped in the curves. Cut along the line for the mouth.
6. Turn the puppet right side out and you are ready to put on the face and hair, etc.
7. Cut out the mouth from pink or red cloth or felt. Sew it in place with tiny
   stitches. First pin the corners so the mouth piece will be straight. You will
   have to stretch the top lip to make it fit the mouth piece. This also makes the
   mouth work better. Stuff the head with cotton above the mouth.
   If you are making the lion, sew on the nose, ears, and tongue. Glue on the eyes
   and nose tip. Stitch on fringed yarn or fur for his mane, and you have a lion.

a bear

a dog

This puppet
can be people
too, such as
a clown or
a giant or
others.

66

PUPPET BODIES

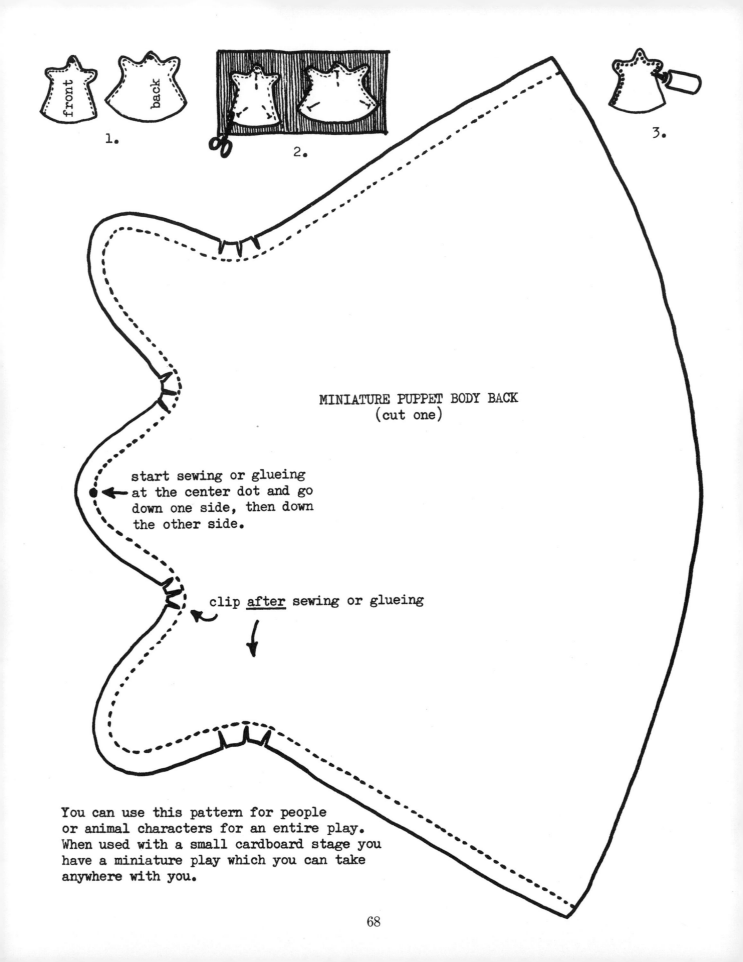

1.

2.

3.

MINIATURE PUPPET BODY BACK
(cut one)

start sewing or glueing
at the center dot and go
down one side, then down
the other side.

clip _after_ sewing or glueing

You can use this pattern for people
or animal characters for an entire play.
When used with a small cardboard stage you
have a miniature play which you can take
anywhere with you.

68

MINIATURE PUPPET BODY

1. Trace the two pattern pieces onto tissue or wax paper and mark the center dot and the words "back" and "front" on them.
2. Place your patterns on your cloth, pin them in place, and cut one back and one front piece.
3. Glue or sew where the dotted lines **are** on the pattern. If you glue, put the glue on in small dots close to the edge of the cloth as shown in step 3. Start glueing at the center dot and go down one side to the bottom and then down the other side. The back piece is supposed to be bigger than the front piece so that it will fit your hand.
4. Clip with your scissors point where the pattern **shows** clips.
5. Turn the puppet body right side out and you are ready to glue on the head. (See HEADS, FACES, and HAIR.)
6. Use this pattern for small characters, such as a mouse, in regular plays or make all your characters by it for a miniature play.

When making animals you can make the front piece a lighter color than the back for a tummy.

MINIATURE PUPPET BODY FRONT
(cut one)

clip _after_ sewing or glueing

Remember!
put the glue on
in a row of tiny dots!

69

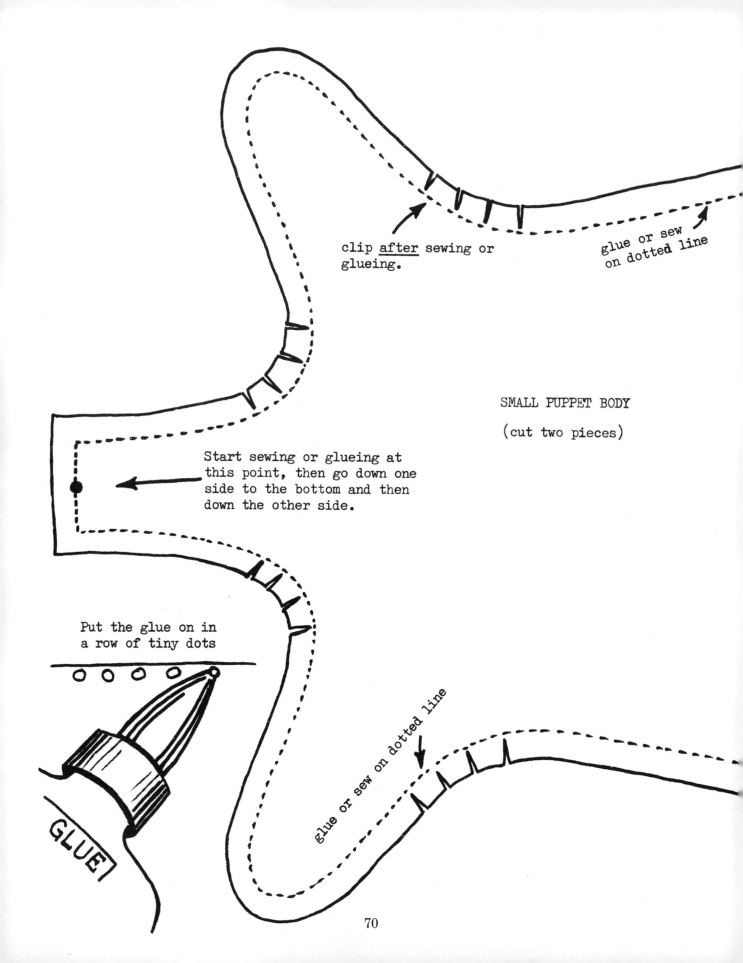

clip _after_ sewing or glueing.

glue or sew on dotted line

SMALL PUPPET BODY

(cut two pieces)

Start sewing or glueing at this point, then go down one side to the bottom and then down the other side.

Put the glue on in a row of tiny dots

GLUE

glue or sew on dotted line

70

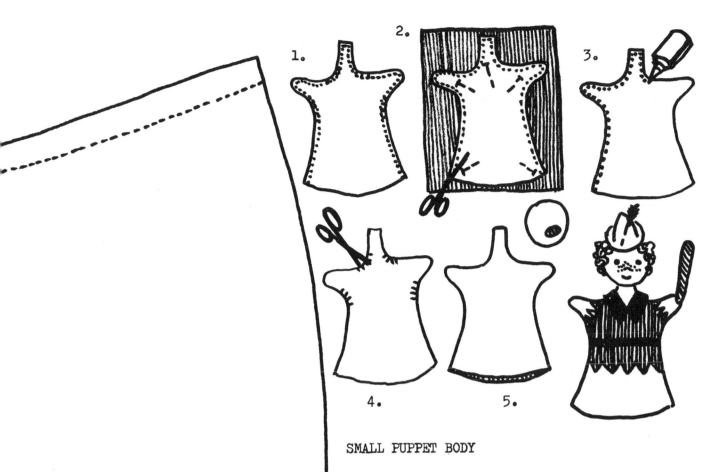

SMALL PUPPET BODY

1. Trace the pattern on tissue or wax paper.
   Cut it out. Be sure to mark seam lines.
2. Pin your pattern to two thicknesses of
   cloth. Cut with scissors.
3. Glue or sew by starting in the middle of the
   neck and going down one side, then the
   other, as shown in step 3. Iron it dry.
4. Clip with scissors point as shown.
5. Turn the body right side out and you are
   ready to glue on the head.
   Place your index finger in the head and
   your thumb and second finger in the arms.
   This size puppet works well with a rod in
   the head as shown. Use a paper tube from
   a coathanger, a new pencil or some other
   dowel.

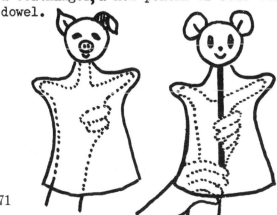

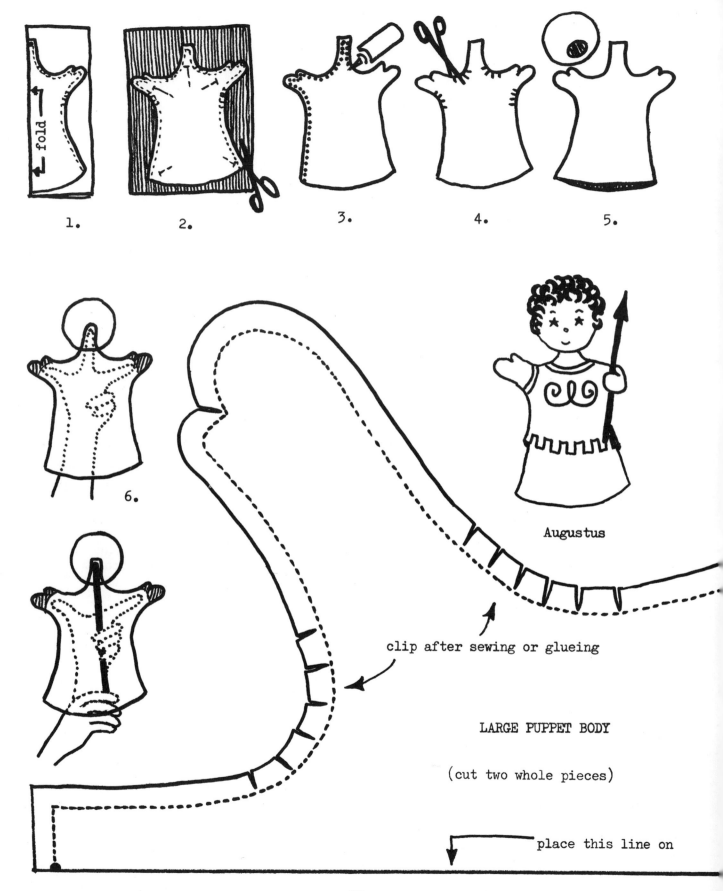

1.

fold

2.

3.

4.

5.

6.

Augustus

clip after sewing or glueing

LARGE PUPPET BODY

(cut two whole pieces)

place this line on

LARGE PUPPET BODY

1. Trace the pattern onto tissue or wax paper or some other paper you can see through. Place the straight center line on the fold of the paper so that when you open it up after cutting, your piece will be a whole pattern.

2. Place your pattern on the cloth and pin it in place. Cut two whole pieces from the cloth. (Do not cut the clips until after the pieces are glued and dry or sewn.)

3. Glue or sew where the dotted lines are on the pattern. If you glue the pieces, put the glue on in a row of tiny dots close to the edge of the cloth. Let it dry, or iron the seams dry in just a few minutes.

4. Clip with your scissors point in the places shown on the pattern.

5. Turn the body right side out and you are ready to glue on the head. Stuff the hands with cotton. Stuff paper or facial tissue up into the neck when you glue the head on to hold it in place. When it is dry take the paper out.

6. Place your index finger in the head and your thumb and second finger in the hands. You can make a hand-and-rod puppet if you like. Use a tube from a coathanger or some other dowel and glue it into the head. Cut it off just at the bottom of the body dress.

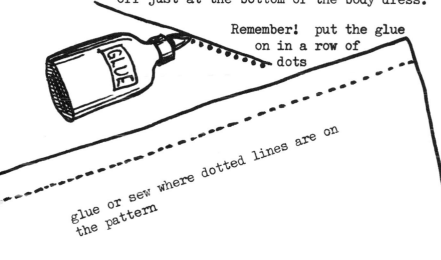

Remember! put the glue on in a row of dots

glue or sew where dotted lines are on the pattern

(This is only half of the pattern. When you trace it, make a whole pattern.)

the fold

This puppet body is good for large or overwhelming characters such as Goliath or Paul Bunyan and others.

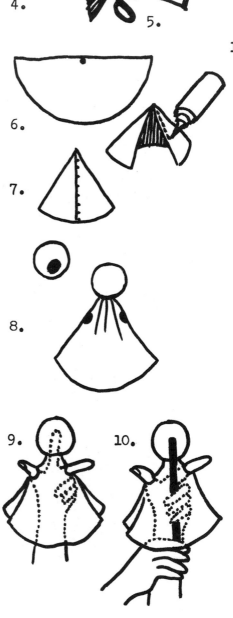

1. Use a rectangle of cloth about 24" x 12" for a large body. Use one about 9" x 18" for a small body or one about 12" x 6" for a miniature body.
2. Fold in half. Mark the center with a dot as shown.
3. Fold it in half again so that it makes a triangle as in step 3.
4. Fold one more time as in step 4.
5. Cut, as in step 5, so that the ends are even.
6. Unfold and you have a half-circle.
7. Fold in the center at the dot and glue the straight edges together as in step 7.
8. Use a styrofoam ball, a stuffed sock toe, an old doll head or some other head. (See pages titled HEADS for ideas.)
9. Place your index finger into the hole in the head and cut two small holes where your thumb and second finger come.
10. This half-circle puppet body works very well with a rod because your thumb and index finger can make even better arms for your puppet than your thumb and second finger can. Your other hand can turn the rod to make the head move and turn in a very realistic way.

For the miniature body use a head about $1\frac{1}{2}$" to 2". For the small body use one about 2" to 3" in diameter, and one about 3" to 4" in diameter for the large size. You can tell if the head is the right proportion for the body by just looking at it; it really isn't necessary to do a lot of measuring. You will want to experiment with different sizes for your own individual puppets.

This body is suitable for a miniature mouse, a small girl pig, a "Marian" and many other characters.

a mouse   a pig   a "Marian" or a mother

HEADS, FACES AND HAIR

MAKE A HEAD FROM THE TOE OF A SOCK!

1. Use an old sock in whatever color you want the puppet's skin to be. Cut the toe off about halfway between the toe and heel as shown.
2. Use cotton, old stockings, facial tissue, or some other kind of stuffing to fill the head.
3. Sew around the bottom leaving a bit of the edge to tuck in later.
4. Draw it up and tie the thread as in step 4. Leave a hole big enough to get your finger into and up into the stuffing.
5. Tuck the edges up into the hole in the head. Be sure the hole is large enough for the puppet's neck to go into it. Try it on your finger and the puppet body to make sure it fits and that the head is the size you want.
6. When you have tried it on and it fits, put glue around the insides of the hole and place it on the puppet body. Stuff tissue or paper into the neck of the body to hold it in place while the glue dries. When dry, remove the paper and you are ready for the face and hair.

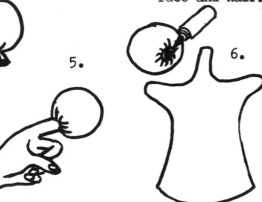

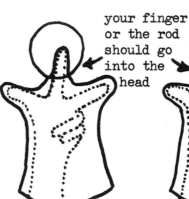

your finger or the rod should go into the head

Use these heads on any of the puppet bodies shown below

any of these can be a rod puppet

large

small

miniature

half-circle puppet

CREATE MANY FACES WITH SOCK HEADS

1. Use a large needle and thread
   to make features by pulling a
   knotted thread through the head
   as shown. Pull the thread through
   where you want the eyes. After
   you make this place for the eyes,
   sew or glue felt or buttons on.
   The tighter you pull the thread
   the deeper the impression in
   the head will be.

2. Beads or wads of cotton can be
   put in the cheeks or chin or
   even the forehead.

3. You can put other things such as
   beads, bottle caps, or spools
   inside for noses.

1.

2.

3.

4. A thread can be pulled through
   to make an impression for the
   mouth. Pull the thread through
   once for a small mouth or several
   times in a row for a wider mouth.
   You can pull the thread very tightly
   to make a deep impression or just
   pull it gently for a different
   effect.

5. Sew or glue beads or buttons
   on the outside. Pin them on
   first to see if you like them,
   then glue or sew them in place.

4.

Real rouge, lipstick, or
crayon can be rubbed on
the cheeks, chin, or
forehead.

5.

Below are some of the characters
from the three plays in chapter 3
made with sock heads.

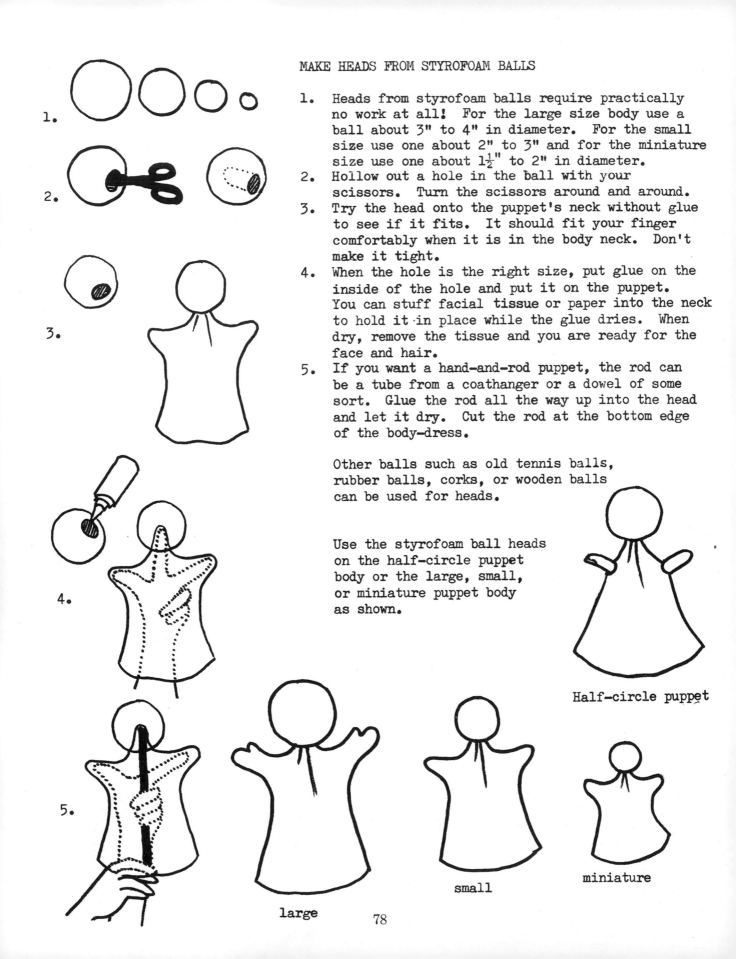

MAKE HEADS FROM STYROFOAM BALLS

1. Heads from styrofoam balls require practically
   no work at all! For the large size body use a
   ball about 3" to 4" in diameter. For the small
   size use one about 2" to 3" and for the miniature
   size use one about 1½" to 2" in diameter.
2. Hollow out a hole in the ball with your
   scissors. Turn the scissors around and around.
3. Try the head onto the puppet's neck without glue
   to see if it fits. It should fit your finger
   comfortably when it is in the body neck. Don't
   make it tight.
4. When the hole is the right size, put glue on the
   inside of the hole and put it on the puppet.
   You can stuff facial tissue or paper into the neck
   to hold it in place while the glue dries. When
   dry, remove the tissue and you are ready for the
   face and hair.
5. If you want a hand-and-rod puppet, the rod can
   be a tube from a coathanger or a dowel of some
   sort. Glue the rod all the way up into the head
   and let it dry. Cut the rod at the bottom edge
   of the body-dress.

Other balls such as old tennis balls,
rubber balls, corks, or wooden balls
can be used for heads.

Use the styrofoam ball heads
on the half-circle puppet
body or the large, small,
or miniature puppet body
as shown.

Half-circle puppet

large

small

miniature

78

FACES ARE EASY ON STYROFOAM BALL HEADS

1. Use felt or cloth scraps for eyes, noses, and mouths. Pin them on first to see how they look, then glue them.
2. You can use buttons and beads too. Sequins and rhinestones give a nice sparkle to the eyes. You can combine felt and button or bead features to make many faces.
3. Use smaller styrofoam balls for noses or ears. Cut them in half for noses, cheeks, or ears as shown.
4. Old stockings or other sheer cloth can be stretched over the styrofoam balls to give color to the faces. Use a cloth which will stretch.
5. Cheeks can be colored with rouge or crayon.
6. Ears can be made by glueing two layers of felt or cloth together. For some animals such as mice, pigs, and cats make the inside of the ears pink.

If you are in a hurry this is the quickest way to make a puppet head.

This is a good kind of head for very young children to learn to make because it is so easy to do.

a woodchopper   a soldier   a girl   a grandmother   "Marian"

YARN BECOMES HAIR

1. Take a piece of yarn and lay it across your puppet's head to see how long to make it. Add an inch or two to be trimmed later.
2. Take a handful of yarn that length. (Use about 25 to 30 strands for small puppets and about 30 to 50 for large puppets.)
3. **Tie** it tightly in the middle as shown.
4. Put this tied yarn across the head and pin it in place. Experiment with it to see how you like it.
5. Spread the strands of **yarn** around to cover the back of the head and sides. The hair-styles below will help you.
   When you are ready to put the hair on to stay, spread glue on the top and down the sides and back of the head. Use pins to help hold hair in place if you need them.
6. Small tufts of yarn tied in the same way make bangs, short hair, and comic hair. You **might** give the puppet a haircut after the glue is dry if he or she needs it!

You can move the part to the side or to the back for side-parts, buns, and so on.

Other materials such as fur, fringe, felt and cloth strips, ball fringe, or real hair can be used for puppet hair.

side-part

boys bangs or side-part

tie it back

(back)

make a bun in back (side)

or on top (side)

pig-tails or braids (back)

buns on sides

straggly, for witches or funny characters

80

COSTUMES

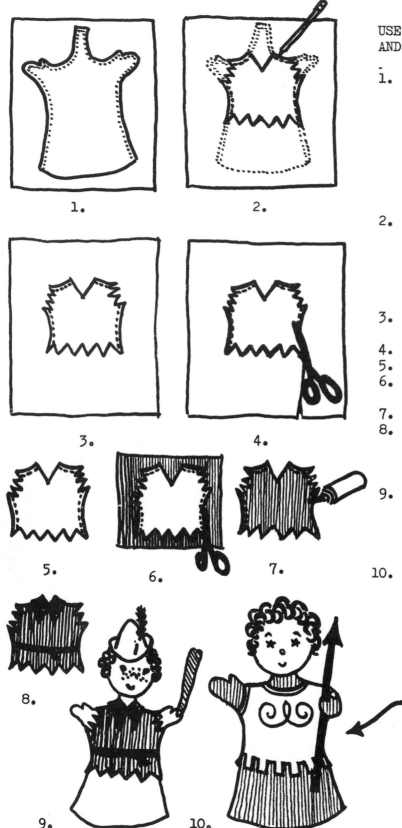

1.

2.

3.

4.

5.

6.

7.

8.

9.

10.

USE THE BODY PATTERNS FOR MAKING
AND DESIGNING YOUR OWN PUPPET COSTUMES

1. The pattern which you used for
   your puppet can also be used for
   clothes. The puppet body dress
   can be the costume itself as shown
   with the "Marian the Librarian"
   puppet. The costume can be made
   separately and slipped on over the
   body as demonstrated here for the
   woodchopper.
2. To make a woodchopper shirt, first
   trace the puppet pattern you used
   for the woodchopper. Draw across
   the arms and across the hips with
   a zig-zag line as shown in step 2.
   Use wax paper or tissue.
3. Draw just the part to be used for
   the shirt as in step 3.
4. Cut your pattern out.
5. Be sure you have the seams marked.
6. Spread the pattern out on two
   thicknesses of cloth and cut.
7. Glue or sew on dotted seam lines.
8. Turn it right side out, add a
   collar and a belt. The collar
   is made from a straight strip of
   cloth.
9. Put the shirt on the puppet by
   slipping it up over the body from
   the bottom. Pull the puppet's
   arms out through the armholes.
   The shirt will stay on by itself.
10. The shirt for the Roman soldiers
    in "The Lion and the Mouse" is
    made in the same way. Gold braid
    was glued on for decoration as
    shown in step 10.

Both puppets have bodies made of
pink cotton cloth. The bodies can
be made in any skin color. The
little shirts can be taken off and
other clothes used to make these
puppets into other characters for
future plays.

There are lots of other little
shirt ideas on the following
pages which you can make by
this method.

82

IT'S SO EASY TO COSTUME YOUR PUPPET
WHEN YOU KNOW HOW!

11. Overalls and aprons are needed in so
    many plays. You make them the same
    way since the hand puppet has no legs
    anyway. The 3rd pig has blue overalls
    made of felt with a pocket glued on to hold
    his bandanna.
12. The 2nd pig is dressed as a girl. The
    same pattern is used for white felt and the
    ruffles are lace. The 1st pig just wears
    a little collar and bow tie.
13. Another apron trimmed with glued-on lace
    is worn by Mother and a little collar
    is all Red Riding Hood's dress needs.
    They both have skin-colored felt hands
    glued on. Red Riding Hood wears a red
    cape and hood made from a half-circle of
    cloth described on another page.
14. Marian's outfit is all sewn together
    with the head glued on. The body and
    the dress are the same and can't come off.
    The body pattern was used for the top part
    which is navy blue and a white pleated
    skirt was sewn on. A collar, made from
    a half-circle, and skin-colored hands
    were glued on.

You will find many doll dresses which
will just fit your puppets. The clothes
for the chubby or baby-type doll work
best because they are big enough in
the waist.

11.

12.

13.

14.

Sometimes, just a bow is all the costume a puppet needs! Or perhaps some trim such as rickrack or braid, or a few patches for a Cinderella. All a king needs is fur trim and a crown. Below are more costumes made with just bits of braid and felt scraps. There are plans for the collars and capes on another page.

Capes can be many different costumes — from a black one for a witch, to an elegant velvet one for a princess. The little apron-overall design shown on another page can be anything from a dainty apron to hillbilly overalls as shown below. These little drawings should start you thinking about all the costumes you can design all by yourself.

No sewing is necessary for these little coats, vests and shirts. Make them of felt
or cloth and glue them. The directions for making a shirt are on another page.
Trim Santa's with cotton or fur, round the front for George Washington, add fringe
for an Indian, or just make a simple vest. Below, you see a Betsy Ross-style dress
made by adding a skirt to the little vest.

A puppet can wear any kind of costume and have any color skin. He can represent
any religious group, nation, or historical period. Puppet plays can tell the
story of your race, religion, or nationality. To make a play fit your social
studies, reading program or art studies, just do a little research and follow
the directions for making puppet costumes.

CLOTHES CAN BE MADE FROM CIRCLES, HALF-CIRCLES, AND QUARTER-CIRCLES

1. A half-circle of cloth can be used for a number of pieces of clothing. Make your circles of paper first and use the paper circle as a pattern.
2. Lay a half-circle across the head for a veil or headcovering as in picture 2.
3. Fasten it under the chin for a cloak as in picture 3.
4. Put a rubber band or a string around the neck for a cape and hood as in picture 4.
5. Cut armholes and you have a coat as in picture 5. This can be worn open or fastened at the neck. Without the holes it can be a cape with a collar.
6. A half-circle with a smaller half-circle cut out as shown in picture 6 makes a long cape, or a short cape, or a collar. You can decorate it, leave it plain, or add a bow.
7. A small half-circle and a string or a ribbon will make a bonnet as in picture 7.
8. A pointed hat can be made from a quarter-circle. Turn it up in back for a woodchopper and add a feather. Turn it up all the way around for a clown hat.
9. A full circle stitched around and gathered makes a nightcap for Grandmother. Many other clothes such as dresses, skirts, aprons, and so on can be made from circles and parts of circles. Cut some paper circles and experiment to see what you can design all by yourself.

The hats can be glued or sewn except for the full circle hat in picture 9. This works best when sewn with a needle and thread.

PROPS AND STAGES

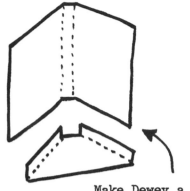

MOST PLAYS NEED AT LEAST ONE PROP

Make Dewey a book to live in. Use cardboard.

Make a shelf of books for Dewey or for a backdrop. It can be pinned to the back curtain or it can stand alone like the one above.

THE END

Announcements such as the title, "Scene I," "THE END," and so on can be put on small signs.

Put hooks or nails just under the stage opening for your props.

Use a narrow box to hold small props which the puppets need to get by themselves or put away during the play.

Use a hairnet, a potato bag, or an orange bag for the Roman soldiers' net.

Use a pencil or some other stick and fringed felt or cloth for brooms and feather dusters.

Use pencils, dowels, or paper tubes from coathangers for the soldiers' spears.

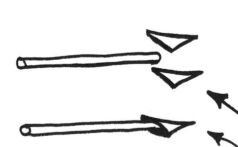

Make the points of two layers of cardboard.

A SMALL SAFETY PIN HOLDS THE PROPS IN PLACE

The woodchopper's club is made with a paper tube or stick covered with felt.

Red Riding Hood's basket can be a small box with a handle glued on and a napkin inside. There are small baskets you can buy.

When you need your hands for other things, your props can hang on the back curtain by themselves. Just use a small size safety pin, a cloth strip and plenty of glue as shown.
If you don't need it , just close the pin until you do.

Be sure the pin points down. Just raise the prop to release the pin.

Make the houses for the 3 Pigs from cardboard. Use two or three thicknesses so that they will be strong. Either draw, paint, or glue on the sticks, straw, and bricks. The rods are paper tubes from coathangers. Glue the rod on with a cloth strip as shown so it won't come off.

You can hang the 2nd pig's feather duster in the house if you like.

The 3rd pig needs to have a fireplace which the wolf can really stick his head in.

back view with pin and rod glued in place

Bundle felt, real sticks, and a paper-covered box for the pigs' building materials.

 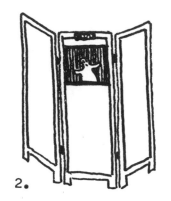 

1.   2.   3.

A FOLDING SCREEN CAN BECOME A SIMPLE LIGHTWEIGHT STAGE

1. Use a folding screen just as it is and stand behind it. Turn the bed lamp so that the light goes up instead of down and that's all you need.
2. You can cut a stage opening in the center panel if you like. Most inexpensive screens are just cardboard inside a wood frame and can be cut with a kitchen knife. (Be sure that you have the permission of an adult to do your own cutting or have an adult cut it for you.)
3. Make the stage just a little bit more professional by putting on curtain brackets and a rod for a back curtain. It can be taken down and folded to put away.

MANY THINGS CAN BECOME HAND-PUPPET STAGES

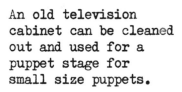  

(back view)

You can set up a temporary stage anywhere with a card table and two blankets or beach towels.

An old television cabinet can be cleaned out and used for a puppet stage for small size puppets.

There are some types of cabinets and chests which can become stages when the back is removed. The best cabinets are the ones with doors. And what's more.....you have drawers to store your puppets and props in!

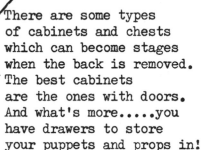

An old firescreen frame can be used for a small size puppet stage placed on the edge of a table. You can cover the frame with cloth or wood and use a bed lamp for light.

add
a small
shelf
and cup
hooks

MAKE A BUILT-IN STAGE IN A CLOSET!

If you have a closet in your own room, a den, or a classroom which you can use, it will make a wonderful stage. Remove part of the panelling or cut a hole in the door, put on a ruffle and a bed lamp and you are ready for a show.

You can put hooks on the back of the door for props and puppets and shelves for storage. You can sit on a low chair as you move the puppets.

1   2   3   4

ANY DOORWAY CAN BE A STAGE

1. A dutch door is perfect for your closet stage or any doorway where you want to give a puppet show.
2. You can install curtain brackets in a doorway and hang a black curtain. Make it a comfortable height so you can sit or stand during your show.
3. If you want something which can be put up and taken down easily you can use those spring-tension, adjustable curtain rods. They don't need screws, nails, or anything.
4. For the easiest stage of all, use a card table on its side in a doorway.

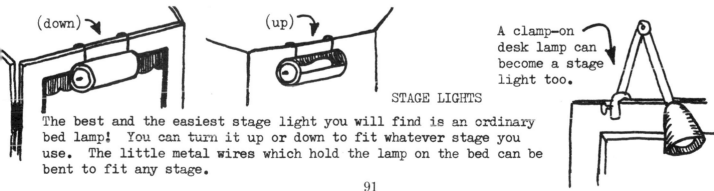

(down)   (up)   A clamp-on desk lamp can become a stage light too.

STAGE LIGHTS

The best and the easiest stage light you will find is an ordinary bed lamp! You can turn it up or down to fit whatever stage you use. The little metal wires which hold the lamp on the bed can be bent to fit any stage.

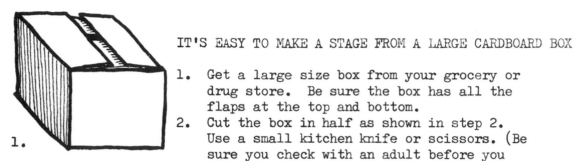

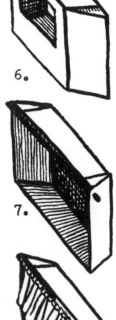

1. Get a large size box from your grocery or drug store. Be sure the box has all the flaps at the top and bottom.
2. Cut the box in half as shown in step 2. Use a small kitchen knife or scissors. (Be sure you check with an adult before you use a knife.)
3. If the flaps are still in place after you finish cutting, pull them loose.
4. Pull the ends of the box around so that the flaps slide out at an angle as in step 4. If your box has printing on it, you can turn it in side out so it will be plain on the outside. Glue it in this position.
5. Trim the edges so the box is even all the way around as in step 5.
6. Spreading the box out like this makes the stage easier to use than if it had straight ends as in step 3.
7. Punch holes in the ends to hold a curtain rod for your back curtain. You can use a real curtain rod, a broomstick, a yardstick or some other rod.
8. You can either hem the curtain over the rod or use clip-on curtain rings. With a line of dots you can glue the hem in the curtain. Make the bottom of the curtain come to just an inch or two below the bottom edge of the stage opening so that you will have room to get your arms underneath.
9. When you cut your stage opening you should cut it nearer the top than the bottom as in step 9. This will allow room for your arms.
10. Decorate your stage any way you like. You can cut flowers from felt or paper and glue them on. You can paint it or cover it with cloth or paper. Perhaps you might like to glue on pictures or draw pictures on it with a felt-tip pen.

Use your stage on the edge of a table as shown in step 10.

Trim the stage opening with a strip of felt cut in scallops, or with a ruffle.

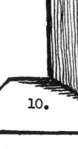

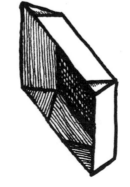

A STAGE CAN TRAVEL!

1. Use a cardboard box which won't slip over your shoulders.
2. Stand up all the flaps. Glue and tape them up. Mark the center of each side, then cut holes to fit your shoulders as shown. They should be at least 6 to 8 inches deep. Try it on and cut out a hole where your face comes.
3. On more cardboard draw around your box for size and make a top 4 or 5 inches bigger all the way around. Glue at least two thicknesses of cardboard together for the top so it will be strong. Glue and tape it onto the box as shown in step 3.
4. Cover the front of the box with a thin black cloth as shown in step 4. Glue it to the front so it will stay in place. Let it extend all the way to the edges of the top. <u>Do not cut out the opening. You look through it.</u>

5. For the cover, cut a piece of cloth to fit the top. Make it about 1 inch bigger all the way around the edges. Hang cloth on all four sides to come to at least below your knees. You can glue and staple the cover to the box or if you can sew, you can make it separate so that it can be taken off to be laundered.
6. After you try it on and mark where the stage opening should be, cut it out. A facing can be sewn or glued on. Fringe or other trim can be sewn or glued on around the opening instead of a facing if you prefer.
   A dowel or stick should be glued or sewn across the bottom edge of the stage opening so it will not sag.

1.

2.

6" to 8"

3.

4.

5.

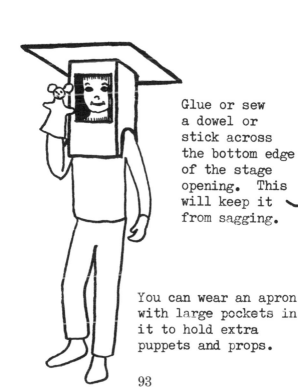

Glue or sew a dowel or stick across the bottom edge of the stage opening. This will keep it from sagging.

You can wear an apron with large pockets in it to hold extra puppets and props.

PUPPET
SHOW
AT
3:00
ROOM 202

6.

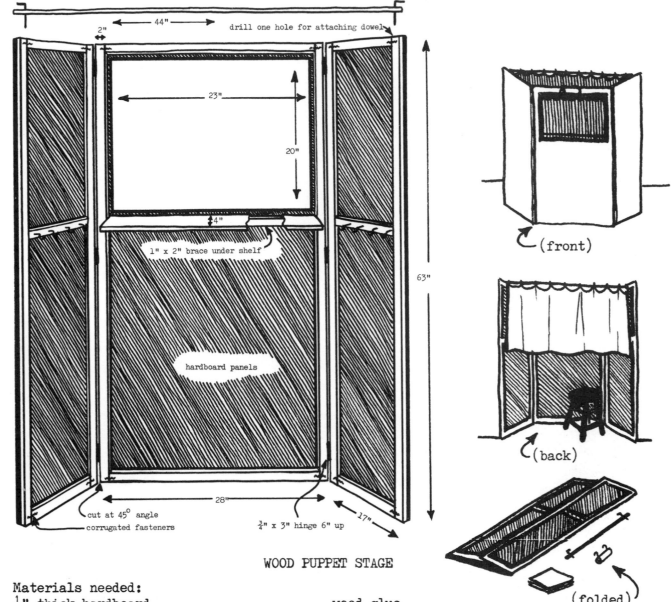

WOOD PUPPET STAGE

Materials needed:

$\frac{1}{8}$" thick hardboard

1" by 2" lumber

$\frac{3}{4}$" diameter dowel and $\frac{3}{4}$" lumber

corrugated fasteners, finishing nails

wood glue

three pair of hinges (6)

finishing materials; sandpaper, paint, etc.

two "L" bolts or large nails

Bill of materials: description	measurements given in inches			special cuts required
	thickness	width	length	
one front panel	$\frac{1}{8}$	28	63	cut out stage opening
two side panels	$\frac{1}{8}$	17	63	
two front vertical frames	1	2	63	angle one edge 45°
four side vertical frames	1	2	63	angle one edge 45° on two
three front cross frames	1	2	25	
six side cross frames	1	2	14	drill holes in two
one dowel	$\frac{3}{4}$ dia.		44	drill two holes
one shelf	$\frac{3}{4}$	4	25	

ABOUT THE AUTHOR

ESTELLE ANSLEY WORRELL worked puppets last summer in the Nashville, Tennessee, Children's Theatre production of "The Golden Goose," which was one of their most successful summer plays. She has also designed costumes for their midwinter play "King Arthur's Sword."

Mrs. Worrell has taught the children's art classes at the Kansas City Art Institute and given puppet shows on TV and in schools and libraries to celebrate such events as National Library Week. She feels that we have only *begun* to realize the educational possibilities of puppetry. Working with children of all ages (including those physically or culturally handicapped), she finds they all respond to and want to participate in a puppet theatre. This book is her answer to that eagerness.

The author received her B.A. in art education from the George Peabody College for Teachers in Nashville. She taught art in Atlanta and later at the Barstow School in Kansas City. Any time she has left from being a wife and the mother of four children, she spends with paints and brushes, needle and thread, pen and ink, or in volunteer work. Her husband, Norman Worrell, is Executive Director of the Tennessee Arts Commission.

In her workshop are three dollhouses with miniature period furnishings and several hundred dolls. Baskets of puppets, paper dolls, and a silk screen press surround her, too, as she creates costumes for forthcoming productions. "Right now I work with words when the house is quiet, and in the afternoons and early evenings we all do visual projects," Mrs. Worrell writes. "Wherever the children are, I am happy to be and to gear my activities to theirs." Her daughters have worked with her in the Children's Theatre and love to give their own puppet shows for other children.